RONALD F. BRIDGES

FIRST LOVE

NAVPRESS

A MINISTRY OF THE NAVIGATORS
P.O. BOX 6000, COLORADO SPRINGS, COLORADO 80934

The Navigators is an international Christian organization. Jesus Christ gave His followers the Great Commission to go and make disciples (Matthew 28:19). The aim of The Navigators is to help fulfill that commission by multiplying laborers for Christ in every nation.

NavPress is the publishing ministry of The Navigators. NavPress publications are tools to help Christians grow. Although publications alone cannot make disciples or change lives, they can help believers learn biblical discipleship, and apply what they learn to their lives and ministries.

© 1987 by Ronald F. Bridges
All rights reserved, including translation
Library of Congress Catalog Card Number:
   87-61182
ISBN 08910-91432

Printed in the United States of America

Contents

Author

Ron Bridges is the Associate Pastor working with youth and Christian education at the First Baptist Church in Golden, Colorado. He served previously at Grace Baptist Church in Glendora, California, and First Baptist Church in Prescott, Arizona. He has also worked with youth ministries in Oregon and Idaho.

He received a B.A. from California Polytechnic State University and an M.A. from Talbot Theological Seminary.

Ron and his wife, Janet, have two sons, Ryan and Tyler, and live in Golden, Colorado.

TO MY LOVELY WIFE, JANET,
WHOSE LIFE AND LOVE CONTINUE TO BE
A GREAT SOURCE OF INSPIRATION TO ME.

Acknowledgments

No one writes a book alone. This book is the result of the input of many different people—from my loving parents to many close friends and teachers—whose lives have served to inspire me toward a greater love for God.

There are a few individuals whose ministries have, in one way or another, made a direct impact on my life, and who have thus contributed toward the writing of this book. Dan DeHaan was the founder and director of "Training Church Leaders" in Atlanta, Georgia, until his accidental death in February, 1982. His perceptive and valuable insights into the Word of God, as well as the example of his devotion to God, served to encourage me through a very difficult time in my own life. He was a man truly in love with his Lord.

To Jon Stine and Don Simpson and the rest of the staff at NavPress I express my sincere appreciation for their support and encouragement to me to write. And my deepest thanks go to Kathy Yanni, whose editorial comments and suggestions were always timely and accurate, and whose friendship I have grown to cherish.

I especially want to thank my loving wife, who freely gave of her time and effort in helping prepare this book. Her love and care saw me through the writing of its pages.

Preface

When the Pharisees heard that [Jesus] had put the Sadducees to silence, they gathered themselves together. And one of them, a lawyer, asked Him a question, testing Him, "Teacher, which is the great commandment in the Law?"

And He said to him, "'You shall love the Lord your God with all your heart, and with all your soul, and with all your mind.' This is the great and foremost commandment."
(MATTHEW 22:34-38)

Our Lord's answer to the lawyer's question is both direct and to the point. Our most important responsibility, our greatest obligation, our number one priority, is to love God with all our heart, soul, and mind—with our whole person!

I remember reading this passage of Scripture as a new Christian and wondering to myself, "How can I love God that much?" The thought boggled my mind to the point that I decided to tuck it away and just begin doing what I had observed other Christians doing. This meant going regularly to church each Sunday, becoming involved in a few activities, and, as often as possible, attending a midweek Bible study.

Over the next several years, I learned much about God and experienced many warm and wonderful times of sincere Christian fellowship. But it wasn't until I was forced into a difficult situation that I was challenged to more fully understand the importance and exciting reality of falling in love with the Lord.

There is a large variety of excellent Bible study and Sunday school materials available for our study today. Many of these materials deal with important peripheral subjects that surround Christianity. But few specifically focus on teaching the believer how to develop and maintain a life-changing love relationship with the God of our universe.

I have prayerfully attempted in this book to provide a glimpse of how a believer can experience such a relationship. My continual prayer is that you might find some of the conclusions and illustrations in these pages beneficial in encouraging you toward a deeper, more intimate love with our Creator.

I have no doubt that once you begin to fully recognize the immeasurable truths of the love of God and the tremendous opportunity freely available to you to draw nearer to Him, you will be inspired to pursue, at all costs, a love relationship with your Lord.

PART I

Developing a Love Relationship

CHAPTER ONE

When Love Is Really Love

*The holiness of God excuses no
sin, but the love of God forgives
all sin through Christ.*
ANONYMOUS

It was just after 10 p.m. when the snow began to fall. A late March storm had moved into our area, bringing with it high winds. An hour earlier, the winds had blown some tree branches into the electrical generator used to power our camp, causing the generator to stop running. The entire grounds were dark except for the center of my staff cabin, where there were two candles burning for our Communion service.

This was a residential camp for adult drug and alcohol treatment situated in the Spring Mountains, some forty miles north of Las Vegas, Nevada. I was working as a substance-abuse therapist after resigning my church ministry position some six months earlier. On this snowy, windy, lonely night, God was about to reveal His love to me in a way I had never before experienced.

* * *

Fresh out of seminary some three years before, I assumed an associate position in Christian education and youth work in a church of about nine hundred members. After about a year, I began to feel unsettled in my job. My love for the ministry was beginning to wane and my love for God did not seem strong enough to motivate me to want to change. I was losing my desire to grow spiritually and I did not know why.

The next six months I began to do things blatantly out of character, such as giving up my personal devotions, not praying much, acting not like a minister but like a man looking out only for himself. My marriage and ministry were being adversely affected. I was putting less and less time into my study and other responsibilities, which was becoming quite evident to the people I worked with.

The next six months proved to be my downfall. Knowing that I was out of the will of God and tampering with sin, I resigned my position. We sold our home and moved back to California. But things continued to worsen. I was angry and bitter, with a cold and hardened heart toward God and my wife. I wanted to get away and be alone.

The next three months, my wife and I had some marriage counseling at her request. The counseling was good, but I had no desire to change. I enjoyed feeling the way I did toward God and my wife, because it was their fault that I had failed in ministry—so I thought.

After reading about a counseling position in the newspaper, I applied and got the job. I had had some counseling classes in seminary, so I thought I could handle it. It seemed that the position would also satisfy my desire to be away, because the job was not in California, but in Nevada.

As a therapist, I was given supervision of nine adults who were in our camp either voluntarily or because of court appointment to our facility. All of them had a history of drug or alcohol abuse.

After I had been on the job a couple of months, a few of my clients learned of my ministry background and approached me with the idea of doing a Sunday church service at the camp. Well, being totally out of fellowship with the Lord and struggling in my marriage, I was in no condition to lead a church service, regardless of where it was. But, not wanting to disclose my backslidden condition, I consented. I prepared the first devotional on the love and grace of God, using John 3:16 and Romans 5:8 as the primary texts. Throughout the planning of that devotional, I felt so uneasy. It had been over six months since I had sincerely opened my Bible.

The following Sunday, I shared a short message with ten clients about the love and grace of God, and His willingness to bestow that love upon us.

I walked away from the service feeling a sense of guilt, something I had not experienced for almost a year. Being insensitive to the Holy Spirit, as well as to my wife and friends, had resulted in a spiritual and emotional numbness that controlled my life. I had been living only for me, for the satisfaction of my desires.

Much to my chagrin, some of the people who had attended Sunday's service asked me to lead a Communion service. Needless to say, I became rather nervous at the idea, remembering that a man must examine himself so as to not take part in the Lord's Supper in an unworthy manner— and I was unworthy. Thus I resisted the very proposal. But during the next week, I was asked three more times. I finally consented. A complicating factor was that I was scheduled to lead the operations of the camp on the coming weekend, something each therapist had to do one weekend per month. The communion service was planned for the Sunday evening of my staff weekend at 10 p.m.

The days leading up to the Communion service were unusual, indeed. I found myself opening up the Bible on several occasions and reading from the book of Psalms. I was calling my wife on the phone every evening. The weekend before the service, Janet flew up to Las Vegas. For the first time in over a year, we thoroughly enjoyed our time together as we talked and explored around Lake Mead.

After Janet left, one of my best friends from my college days came to Las Vegas for a pharmacology convention. Dwight was a friend who did not desert me during these difficult months, even though I was always defensive with him. He came up to the camp to visit me and we talked for several hours about the Lord, my wife, and my ministry.

Just as my wife had done a few days before, Dwight exhibited a true sense of God's love for me. He spoke of his personal concern for my well-being, as well as God's tremendous love and forgiveness for all His children.

My cold and hardened heart was gradually beginning to thaw. I kept thinking about the things Dwight had said, the special weekend Janet and I had experienced, and the Sunday service I had led two weeks before.

Soon, my weekend arrived. It went along as usual, except for a knife fight I had to help break up between two clients. Also, I found contraband on another man, which meant that I had to dismiss him from camp—at 1:30 a.m.

* * *

Sunday evening arrived, along with the Pacific storm we had been expecting for a couple of days. At ten o'clock, eight of us gathered on the dirty wooden floor of my cabin, dressed in heavy clothing. We huddled around two burning candles and prepared for the service.

After reading John 15:1-13, I asked the people in the group to share about their lives and to express something they needed to change in their relationship with God. It was a time I will never forget. Here was a group of people who had done or committed just about every ungodly act imaginable—and yet they were sincerely humbling themselves before God, sharing from their hearts, seeking God's forgiveness. This was not just a remorseful time of testimony, but rather a powerful time of observing God's great love and exalted holiness moving in on repentant hearts— including my own.

It was at last my turn to share. I began by sharing with the group about the truth of my past. Before I could get very far, I had to stop. As I broke down and cried, Earl, a man who had recently kicked a nineteen-year addiction to heroin, reached over and put his arm around me and reminded me that God loved me very much and would forgive me. He then added that I should quit the camp and get back to my wife and get back in ministry. All at once God's forgiving love broke through like a tidal wave. I realized that it was time to go back home.

I spent the rest of that night on my knees with the Lord. For the first time in my life, I truly experienced the depth of God's love through His forgiveness. I reread John 15 and discovered the truth that had escaped me for so long. As I thought back on the previous twelve months of my life, I realized that God had been taking me through the pruning process mentioned in John 15:2-11. My love for Him had to be changed. I needed to open my eyes to the importance of having and maintaining a deep, intimate walk with Him. In our relationship with God, the unifying element is love. The result of such a love relationship is obedience and joy.

It's not that I had been confused about what love was. I understood God's love as our supreme example. What I had lacked was the depth and power of His love in my life. As a result, when the struggles of my marriage and ministry began to affect me, I progressively weakened by dropping my spiritual guard step by step. A person who comes to the point of being totally insensitive to God does so not by one giant leap but through small individual steps. Each step in the wrong direction gets easier because the steps before it were not really so drastic.

Because my motivation for loving God was based on just a strong affection (for I had never really experienced His true love), my step-by-step walk toward sin and a hardened heart was not halted. If someone had asked me, "Do you love God?" I would have replied, "Well, *of course* I love God!" But my love was not the kind of love that evolves directly from the Lord. It was a self-serving, self-seeking love that looked good on the surface but was not at all pleasing to God. I was a Christian, but like Peter, as we will see later, I had a misconception of what kind of love God desired from me.

It is God's love (the Greek word is *agapē*) for us that defines what our response of love to Him should be. *Agapē* love can be given to God only when it has first been received from God. The apostle John reminds us:

Every one who loves is born of God and knows God. . . . By this the love of God was manifested in us, that God has sent His only begotten Son into the world so that we might live through Him. In this is love, not that we loved God, but that He loved us and sent His Son to be the propitiation for our sins. (1 John 4:7,9-10)

Our love for God must be strong enough to cause us to endure for His glory. Our love for Him should motivate us to spend time loving Him through our prayer, devotion, and worship, regardless of how busy our schedules may be or how active we are in doing things "for Him" through our church activities. It must be a love that reflects the traits and qualities of His love without compromise.

Perhaps one of the most vivid and poetic descriptions of God's love comes from A.W. Tozer in his book *The Knowledge of the Holy*:

> His love is an incomprehensibly vast, bottomless, shoreless sea before which we kneel in joyful silence and from which the loftiest eloquence retreats confused and abashed.[1]

We cannot respond with a deep, intimate love for the Father until we have first received and understood the power of His supreme love for us through the sacrifice of His Son. This was God's ultimate sacrifice, and it is our primary example of true love (1 John 4:9-10).

DISCERNING WHAT MOTIVATES US

Understanding our motives will help clarify significantly our love for God. We may sometimes convince ourselves that our love for God is truly love because of what we publicly do or say. If so, we are deceiving ourselves. As Francois de la Rochefoucauld has said, "There is only one kind of love, but there are a thousand imitations." It is essential that we stop and think through our true motives for loving God. We must ask ourselves, Why do we do what we do, and for whose gain?

People have many different motives in life: to get ahead, to stay ahead, to make our moms and dads happy, to make ourselves happy, and so forth. These are the deep ambitions behind our will, the wind behind our sails, the feelings behind our actions.

A motive is something that incites us to action. Thus, our motives are established as a result of what we decide is important. *What we decide is important* is indeed the key. For if our love for God is truly love, then our motives will reflect a heart for God. If our love for Him is anything less than true *agapē* love, then our motives have a much greater potential to become merely ambitions of the flesh.

Our Lord, in His Sermon on the Mount, said, "Where your treasure is, there will your heart be also" (Matthew 6:21). Our Lord certainly knows the heart of man. What our heart deems important, we will establish motives to pursue. Therefore, if we truly value God's presence with us as our only treasure, our motives will center around our daily walk with God and the things of God. Our motives will always distinguish a hypocritical love from a true love.

Our Lord did not use the titles of the religious leaders of Israel (Pharisees, Sadducees, scribes, and so on) when He referred to them. He preferred the term "hypocrites." Speaking of their motives, Jesus said:

> "Woe to you, scribes and Pharisees, hypocrites! For you clean the outside of the cup and of the dish, but inside they are full of robbery and self-indulgence. . . . Even so you too outwardly appear righteous to men, but inwardly you are full of hypocrisy and lawlessness." (Matthew 23:25,28)

On one occasion, Jesus was even more blunt:

> "You are those who justify yourselves in the sight of men, but God knows your hearts; for that which is

highly esteemed among men is detestable in the sight of God." (Luke 16:15)

Jesus was criticizing the scribes and Pharisees for their hypocrisy. They claimed to love God, but they didn't really love Him as much as they loved themselves and their positions before men. The motives of their hearts were full of hypocrisy and lawlessness.

Before we single out the Pharisees, scribes, and Sadducees, we must stop and consider our own motives. Do we "love" God in order to be seen by men? Do we do things in our church to be recognized by others as loving God?

Hypocrisy is surely a proven indicator of improper motives. It is also one of the most devastating elements of spiritual warfare that we should battle against on the evangelistic front. I believe more harm is done to the advancement of the gospel by one hypocritical Christian than by a thousand nonbelievers cursing the faith.

As Christians, it is very easy for us to be led by improper motives that are only for self-gain if we are not on guard, mindful of the presence of God in our lives. For example, it is easy to stop the pastor after services and tell him what a great message he gave, even though we do not remember any of it. Or, how about being overly complimentary to everyone in order to solicit the same from them or at least restrict their criticism of us?

Perhaps you consider these examples only "minor" improper motives. But one small step leads to another, and before you realize it, your motivations are only for self-gain. Soon your love for God is no longer being expressed to Him but is being paraded before men with a spiritual pride that will eventually show its true colors. Improper motives resulting from a weak love relationship with God can result in all sorts of spiritual problems. Our heart must be a one-master heart, exclusively in love with the Lord. There can be no room for a second master.

HOW DO WE KNOW IT IS LOVE?

Before we can evaluate our love for God, we must first evaluate our *reasons* for loving God. These reasons will dictate our motivations, which will in turn determine the quality and intensity of our love toward God.

Such an approach in determining our "kind" of love for the Lord is similar to Jesus' approach in questioning Peter regarding his "kind" of love for Him (John 21:15-17). This encounter between Jesus and Peter is a good illustration for us because we can identify with so many of Peter's weaknesses. He was a man full of mistakes and God did not cover them up. But even though Peter had failed our Lord, he could still have a love relationship with Him.

On several occasions, Peter had boasted about his commitment to Jesus, but the Lord had enough insight into Peter's character to know that his love for God had to be modified and strengthened through a pruning process. Peter set himself up for pruning when he boasted one day to the Lord that even though others might fall away in their commitment, he would not. "Even if I must die with You, I will not deny You" (Matthew 26:35).

Initially, Peter was true to his word. Just a short time after his statement of commitment, he was boldly standing between Jesus and the soldiers who had come to arrest Him, with sword drawn defending his Lord. But a short time after that, our hero Peter denied knowing Jesus three times before a slave girl and others who were accusing him of being a disciple of Jesus. Just then, when he realized what he had done, Peter went out and wept bitterly.

The Lord wanted to prune Peter's life by helping him see that his love for God was not the kind of love that would motivate him enough to endure under great pressure. Peter's love for God was a mixture of truth and personal prestige. He had a strong affection (*philia*) for the Lord, but not a love (*agapē*) that was mature, all-encompassing, all-enduring, and self-sacrificing.

Jesus wanted to make sure Peter realized what it truly meant to *love* God and what it would cost him, so He went right to the heart of the problem, questioning Peter three times about his love for Him:

> When they had finished breakfast, Jesus said to Simon Peter, "Simon, son of John, do you love Me more than these?" He said to Him, "Yes, Lord; You know that I love You." He said to him, "Tend My lambs."
>
> He said to him again a second time, "Simon, son of John, do you love Me?" He said to Him, "Yes, Lord; You know that I love You." He said to him, "Shepherd My sheep."
>
> He said to him the third time, "Simon, son of John, do you love Me?" Peter was grieved because He said to him the third time, "Do you love Me?" And he said to Him, "Lord, You know all things; You know that I love You." Jesus said to him, "Tend My sheep." (John 21:15-17)

On the surface, our Lord's questioning appears redundant. But a check of the Greek text reveals that Jesus used two different terms for "love" here. In His first two questions to Peter, He used the verb *agapaō* for love. In His third question, and in all three of Peter's replies, the verb *phileō* is used for love.

The term *agapaō* connotes the idea of a deep, sincere, intimate, selfless love for another. It appears in John 3:16, where it is used of divine love that has a sense of preciousness of the love object. The term *phileō* connotes mainly emotional warmth and attachment, implying fondness or strong friendship. It reflects a delighted affection for the love object.

Most theologians see the change of terms in this context as very noteworthy. The *New International Version* translates *agapaō* here as "truly love" and *phileō* as simply "love." This is a significant distinction, one that will have a profound effect in our attitude toward God, especially when difficult times come. This was precisely the point of our Lord's questioning of Peter. He was seeking to probe Peter's motivation for following Him, showing him that his strong affection for God needed to be strengthened. Only a complete love for Christ would be sufficient to enable Peter to endure the difficult trials that awaited him.

Peter was grieved at Jesus' third question because he knew that when He used *phileō* for love, He was challenging Peter's love and questioning its genuineness. Perhaps this was the final clipping in the Lord's pruning of Peter, for every time we see him in the book of Acts, he is a man full of power, motivated by an intense love for God. Every time Peter writes the word "love" in his Epistles, he uses the term *agapē*. This is significant because Peter was writing to Christians who were facing the atrocities of Nero's persecutions, in which thousands of Christians were put to death for their love and faith in the living God, the Lord Jesus Christ. If there ever was a time for people to prove their *agapē* love for God and to endure, it was then. For they truly had to experience a deep in-love relationship with God in order to give up their lives for the sake of His Name.

An important point must be made here. We are believers with the indwelling of the Holy Spirit, who has given us a spirit of power, discipline, and the love of God (Romans 5:5,

2 Timothy 1:7). Thus we must make a conscious effort to know and understand the love of God through His Word (1 John 2:5). It must be a disciplined act of the will to generate an in-love response to the Father. It will not just happen on its own. In his passionate prayer to God, Moses asked, "If I have found favor in Thy sight, let me know Thy ways, that I may know Thee, so that I may find favor in Thy sight" (Exodus 33:13). God answered this prayer as a result of Moses' sincere heart request to *know* Him. This must likewise be our supplication if we desire a deep, intimate love relationship with the Father. We must *want* to seek such a relationship.

Try to place yourself in Peter's position, standing before Christ as He asks you three times, "Do you love Me?" Could you respond without hesitation, "Yes, Lord, I truly love You," being aware as you say it of your current interests and motivations? How long could you have endured during Nero's persecutions or any of the other persecutions of the early Church? Would you like to have an idea of how you would do? If so, then try the following test: Check yourself the next time your teacher in class, co-worker at work, or relatives at home ridicule the gospel and mock your heavenly Father. What, if any, is your response? The Christians in Peter's day responded in God's strength and love without yielding, even though almost certain death was their sentence for doing so. Why? Because their faith was unshakable through their *agapē* love for Him.

Is such a commitment too much for us to consider? If our love for God is truly love, shouldn't there be some evidence of our commitment? But what if we are living in a continually weakened spiritual condition? Perhaps our motivation is weak or deluded as a result of a merely affectionate or misunderstood love for God. Our motivation will certainly confirm our heart's intent.

A good friend of mine went through a painful experience several years ago as a result of developing the wrong motives for loving God. Jerry and I became friends through our church's college-career group. This group was a real source of spiritual challenge and growth. It was also well attended and very active. Jerry's involvement with our group was always one of high exposure. He placed himself in situations that would cause others to comment, "My, isn't Jerry faithful?" or, "Isn't Jerry a wonderful Christian?" He was always doing things in the church that caught the attention of many.

There was an emotional side to Jerry that only a few of us in the group were aware of. Jerry's feelings were easily hurt when he was not appreciated enough. He complained that he was always taken for granted, which seemed to cause him to do things bigger and better. His motivation for doing things in the church was fueled by his need to feel wanted and appreciated.

After a few years, Jerry met a wonderful young lady who was faithfully committed to the Lord. She came from a family with a background of men serving faithfully in the ministry. During their engagement, Jerry proudly announced that after their marriage, he would attend seminary and go into the ministry. Everyone praised his decision and wished him well. His bride-to-be and her family were so proud of Jerry. He felt on top of the world.

Three months after their wedding, Jerry and his wife left town to attend seminary many miles away. Once there, almost immediately Jerry began to struggle. They knew no one in the town they settled in. Jerry's security in what he did for the Lord and accolades from other people were no longer there. There was no one to pat him on the back. Soon, Jerry became disillusioned with Christianity, claiming that no one cared about him. The relationship between him and his wife began to deteriorate. He blamed many of his negative feelings on her. He felt that her "Christianity" and her family background placed expectations on him that pressured him into going to seminary. After his first semester, he dropped out of seminary with bitter feelings and went to work as a salesman.

Now, six years later, Jerry has renewed his love for his wife and has discovered the joy of an in-love relationship with God. He is working as a salesman and he and his wife are actively involved in their church. Jerry now has a different motive. He is a servant with a heart for God.

I had an opportunity to spend some time recently with Jerry. We had not seen each other for several years. He shared with me where he felt he went wrong. He reminded me how he had always been so busy doing things in the church. At that time he felt a great responsibility to live up to the expectations of his wife and her relatives.

Jerry said that now he didn't blame anyone but himself. He had been trying to be someone he was not—on his own power. He was now able to recognize that his behavior was caused by his misconception of true love for God, which in turn resulted in wrong motives. He had loved God because people patted him on the back, because people said, "Jerry is a fine Christian." His love for God was like his love for personal recognition. He had not learned how to truly love God without an ulterior motive.

Our reasons for loving God must be, first and foremost, grounded in God Himself. Jesus called it the foremost commandment: "Hear, O Israel; The Lord our God is one Lord; and you shall love the Lord your God with all your heart, and with all your soul, and with all your mind, and with all your strength" (Mark 12:29-30).

This passage will clarify for us what qualifies as true love. What are our motives for loving God? Are they a result of what God does for us? Are they a result of what God might do for us? Are they a result of what an identification with God will do for us?

To answer these questions on a personal level, try the following suggestion: Write down all the reasons why you presently love God. Then observe what you have written, asking yourself, "Are my reasons for loving God a result of what He does or what I am hoping He will do?" Do you say, "I love God because . . ." or "I love God if . . ."? These statements may suggest improper motives. For example, I love God *because*. . . . Because of what? Because He answers my prayers; because He makes me feel good; because I am popular in the church.

But what happens when He doesn't answer your prayers as you wish? What happens when He doesn't make you feel good? A love based on "because" (other than "because He first loved me") attaches conditions to our love. With such love, we will not stand strong when the Lord allows trials to come into our lives.

What if we love God only *if* . . . ? If what? If He will bring me a husband; if He will take all my problems away; if He will help with my finances. But our love for God must have *no* conditions. Here's how we should state our love for God: "I love the Lord with all my heart, soul, mind, and strength, *regardless* of. . . ." Such love is not attached to any peripheral circumstances or conditions. We love God as He first loved us: unconditionally. This is the proper motive for loving God.

Take some time out of your schedule to spend alone with God. Ask the Lord for insight into your motives for loving Him. Is your love a mature *agapē* love? A love based on no conditions?

Here's how the apostle John described the motive in the hearts of some faithful traveling missionaries: "They went out for the sake of the Name, accepting nothing from the Gentiles. Therefore we ought to support such men, that we may be fellow-workers with the truth" (3 John 7-8). For our love to mature in quality and intensity, our only motive must be "for the sake of the Name." Then what we do is based on Him and Him only, and we show our love for Him with a passion that goes far beyond an affection. It is a love that understands no limits, restrictions, or conditions.

NOTES:
1. A.W. Tozer, *The Knowledge of the Holy* (San Francisco: Harper & Row, 1961), page 105.

CHAPTER TWO

Why a Love Relationship?

What we love we shall grow to resemble.
BERNARD OF CLAIRVAUX

Hardly a day passes by without the word *love* popping up in conversation, songs, and commercial advertising all around us. "I love the weather"; "She loves the opera"; "You'll love our sale"; "Doug loves Mary." We use the word in a variety of ways to convey a variety of meanings.

From television commercials to greeting cards, the commercial marketplace has certainly made use of this word to fit whatever it desires to communicate. I recently saw a television commercial showing a man pampering his car with a certain automotive product. Apparently the product requires extra time to apply, so the key to the commercial was the concluding statement: "After all, when you're in love, what's a few extra minutes?" If you are really in love with your car the extra time will allegedly not bother you.

Greeting cards are based on the idea of people communicating love in various situations and circumstances. The methods used for communicating love are various indeed. One card may do so with a compassionate poem, while another may utilize satire and humor.

I will never forget the greeting card a friend of mine in college got for a former girlfriend after she dropped him. It read, "Your love used to cause tingles to race up my spine. But then, so does scratching my fingernails on a chalk-board."

Because "love" is used in so many different ways to communicate a variety of meanings, it has been misused, stretched, and watered down to fit our ever-changing feelings and desires.

But the word "love" holds an especially profound and significant place within Christianity. Many theologians would agree that love is the central theme throughout the Bible. It is at the very heart of God's dealings with man. Therefore, it is not surprising that much has been written about love, especially regarding our responsibility to love our neighbor. But what is surprising is the fact that very little has been written clearly defining our personal responsibility in loving God and the benefits resulting from such a relationship. Perhaps we take for granted our responsibility, never looking beyond our own personal definition of love (which may or may not be a biblical definition, especially if our definition has become saturated with a variety of meanings).

It is becoming increasingly apparent that the overuse and misuse of the word "love" has crept into Christian circles rather unnoticed. Lack of spiritual maturity and commitment has given rise to our misunderstanding of love, allowing us to be comfortable with a weaker definition that requires little sacrifice or commitment. As a result, *love* has become the hackneyed term of a generation of Christians who combine their love for God with their love for their favorite car, food, or sporting event. Consequently, their "love" for God provokes no more motivation and intensity than their joy in seeing their favorite baseball team (which they "love") win a big game.

We attend church and listen to our minister describe God's love for us and His desire for us to love Him in return. But because our concept of *true* love is weak, we are not motivated toward a deeper love and commitment toward Him.

If our relationship with God is in such a weakened condition, it is because our misunderstanding of His love has resulted from one of two reasons: (1) We have never really experienced God's love or (2) our understanding of love is so confused that we have no idea how to apply it in our relationship with God. If we suffer from either one of these problems, then we need to seriously evaluate our walk with God by focusing on our concept of love. We must place our definition of love alongside God's supreme demonstration of genuine love by the sacrifice of His only Son for our salvation.

If we are to grow and mature spiritually and to endure through the many pains of life, our motivation to complete our pilgrimage here on earth must be rooted in a deep, sincere love relationship with the Father. Such a love is far greater than our love for certain foods or clothes or any other peripheral item we may treasure. It is an all-encompassing love, a love that demands of us a degree of intensity no person or earthly circumstance could ever produce.

It is this intensity that our Lord attempted to communicate to the Pharisees in His response to their question about the greatest commandment: "'You shall love the Lord your God with all your heart, and with all your soul, and with all your mind.' This is the great and foremost commandment" (Matthew 22:37-38).

LOVE OR INFATUATION?

The concept of *falling in love* is universal. We use the phrase "falling in love" to describe an occurrence in one's life that promotes changes. These changes, most of us would agree, are in the seat of the emotions: the heart, mind, and soul within. Such changes motivate our actions to respond to the object of our love.

How could we ever forget our first love in our youthful days: the nervous excitement, the butterflies in the stomach, the sweaty palms and weak knees? But was it even love? Was it perhaps just infatuation? The words *love* and *infatuation* describe conditions that appear similar on the surface, but are vastly different. Infatuation is sparked by the visible: things that are attractive to our physical senses. Love is spawned and nourished mostly by the invisible: those traits and attributes that can be viewed only through a deep, intimate knowledge of another person. Infatuation can certainly lead to love, but it must be nurtured along to see beyond the visible, to become morally discerning and dying to self.

This is why "true" love demands a period of time, allowing knowledge and trust to grow. Such love is based not on fleeting sentiment resulting from excited, physical senses, but on a knowledge discerned and developed through deep understanding. Paul alluded to true love and some of its genuine characteristics in his prayer for the church at Philippi: "This I pray, that your love may abound still more and more in real knowledge and all discernment,

so that you may approve the things that are excellent"
(Philippians 1:9-10).

Falling in love with the Lord does not occur overnight,
but over time. It is a sincere response from the seat of our
emotions to the *agapē* love bestowed on us by the Father. It
is not a condition for salvation, but an aspect of our daily
walk with Him after salvation. Such a response will motivate
us toward a higher degree of personal spiritual commitment, a commitment that is not established through obligation or visible reinforcement but based on the response of
an obedient and loving heart to its Lover, our heavenly
Father.

When we are brand new Christians, our love toward
God may be an infatuation or strong affection but not a true
love since our knowledge of Him has not had time to root
itself into a close, intimate friendship. We are certainly
children of God at the point of our conversion, but we must
mature in our knowledge and love of Him.

A new baby is a living illustration of this truth. A baby is,
in a sense, an adult even at birth. It merely lacks maturity. It
is born with everything it will have as an adult. It does not
grow eyes and ears later on, but it is born with them. The
only thing lacking at birth is the mental, physical, and
emotional maturity of an adult. The more it learns, the
more it matures.

Our love for God runs a similar course. It is not mature
at our conversion, but the more we know of Him, the more
our love matures. Therefore, an important factor in our
spiritual growth is our conscious effort to know God intimately, learning about His ways and understanding His
love. We gradually learn how to respond to Him with the
same kind of love that He has shown us. We do so in our
intimate devotion and worship.

The great byproduct of such a relationship is our ability to begin seeing and understanding things from God's perspective. Accordingly, we learn to trust totally in His sovereignty, enabling us to endure not only through the everyday trials of life but also through the major tribulations that will come. This is one of the promises couched in Paul's instruction to us in Romans 8:28: "We know that God causes all things to work together for good to those who love [*agapaō*] God. . . ."

A man who understands his love for God does not worry about what may lie ahead. For he lives not in fear, but in love. "There is no fear in love; but perfect love casts out fear, because fear involves punishment, and the one who fears is not perfected in love" (1 John 4:18).

THREE MEN WHO TRULY LOVED GOD

There are many accounts down through history of God's involvement with men and women who, because of their love relationship with Him, became mighty examples to their generation. Three men in particular, two from Bible times and one contemporary, are certainly representative of people with an extraordinary conviction of love and loyalty toward God. Because of this strength of commitment, they were able to face social mockery and death without wavering. They were merely ordinary men whose fervent love for their God made them extraordinary men of faith and endurance.

Noah—Noah was "a righteous man, blameless in his time." He "walked with God" (Genesis 6:9). The phrase "walked with God" refers to the intimate spiritual and loving relationship Noah experienced with God. This relationship was not a one-time occurrence, but a consistent, faithful lifestyle. Noah developed such a lifestyle, enabling him to endure through the evil generation in which he lived.

Noah responded in total obedience out of his faith in

God to a difficult, seemingly impossible task. Noah's assignment was to build an ark, something he had never seen or heard of before. The social pressure he received while building it made his task even more difficult. Yet without question, he responded in total obedience to God's command.

Noah was a man whose heart was totally devoted to the One he loved. Therefore, to do the impossible was possible; to face the social pressure was bearable; to trust God completely was feasible.

When God gives us clear direction in a matter, why is it that our first inclination is to do what we want instead of what He wants? I firmly believe that such disobedience is a result of how we view God in our heart. Is our love for Him strong enough to cause us to totally trust and commit our lives to His leading? It certainly was in Noah's heart. Noah's love for God was so intense that there was absolutely no room for doubt.

As a result of Noah's faithfulness, God delivered him from death and honored him with an everlasting covenant. Noah's relationship with God was reflected in the character of the man of wisdom in Proverbs 8:32-35:

> "Now therefore, O sons, listen to me [wisdom], for
> blessed are they who keep my ways. Heed instruction
> and be wise, and do not neglect it. Blessed is the man
> who listens to me, watching daily at my gates, waiting
> at my doorposts. For he who finds me finds life, and
> obtains favor from the LORD."

Stephen—We first learn of Stephen in Acts 6. He was one of the seven disciples chosen to serve tables, though he soon became a powerful preacher whose intense love for God cost him his life.

The description of Stephen in Scripture begins with the word "full." He was full of power, full of grace, full of wisdom, full of faith, and full of the Holy Spirit.

Unable to cope with Stephen's wisdom, Jews from "the Synagogue of the Freedmen" (Acts 6:9) stirred up the people against him by spreading slanderous comments about what he was preaching. As a result, the people came to Stephen and dragged him before the Sanhedrin. It was before that council that Stephen, in his fervent love for God, delivered his remarkable apologia, which would eventually lead to his death. As this proclamation of Stephen's faith concluded, the Lord opened Stephen's eyes to allow him to gaze intently into heaven, where he saw "the glory of God, and Jesus standing at the right hand of God" (Acts 7:55).

Stephen's description of this incredible vision caused the council to cry out with a loud voice and cover their ears. As Stephen continued to speak, they rushed him out of the city and began to stone him. Stephen was full of love, not only for his heavenly Father but also for his own murderers. He cried out in a loud voice as the stones were pelting his body, "Lord, do not hold this sin against them!" (Acts 7:60). Only a man with a deep, intimate love for God could ever respond as Stephen did.

You say, "I don't think I'm ready for that yet." Well, I'm not suggesting that developing such a love relationship with God will end with similar results. The point is that Stephen reminds us that our lives are in God's hands and that He chooses to do with us as He wills. Our mark of love for Him is to be a glory to Him—through our endurance or even through our death. If our love relationship brings tremendous persecution, as it did with Stephen, then to God be the glory.

Let us not forget Peter's exhortation to the saints who were suffering during Nero's persecutions: "After you have suffered for a little, the God of all grace, who called you to His eternal glory in Christ, will Himself perfect, confirm, strengthen and establish you" (1 Peter 5:10).

Chet Bitterman—Chet Bitterman was a young man who gave his life for the sake of the Name. Kidnapped by terrorists who were hoping to force the Summer Institute of Linguistics (a part of Wycliffe Bible Translators) out of their country, Bitterman was held for ransom, which ended in his murder.

Wycliffe Bible Translators and the Summer Institute of Linguistics were founded by W. Cameron Townsend and L.L. Legters in 1934. Since then, WBT and SIL have been providing the Word of God for many different language groups throughout the world. Working with the Caryona-speaking Indians in Colombia was just another outreach of their ministries. Chet Bitterman was given the task of bringing the gospel to these Indians in their native language.

Arriving in the summer of 1979 with his wife Brenda, who was pregnant with their second child, the Bittermans were unsuccessful in their attempt to begin work with three other language groups. Then they made arrangements to go to the Caryona-speaking Indians, when Chet suddenly became ill and was sent to Bogota for medical evaluation. It was determined that he needed gall bladder surgery. While staying at the SIL headquarters awaiting surgery, his kidnapping occurred.

Terrorists disguised as policemen knocked on the door at 6:30 a.m. When the door was opened, six terrorists, hooded and armed with machine guns, rushed in. They were looking for Al Wheeler, director of the Bogota SIL office. When they could not find him, they instead chose Chet Bitterman, apparently because he seemed to be in charge.

Four days later, the terrorists made their demands:

"Chet Bitterman will be executed unless the Summer Institute of Linguistics and all its members leave Colombia by 6:00 p.m. February 19."[1]

After several previous attacks on missionaries throughout Latin America, Wycliffe members had voted in 1975 that the mission would not yield to terrorists' demands. It was that statement of policy that prevented WBT and SIL from even considering submitting to the demands of Chet's captors.

For the next forty-eight days, the many attempts to negotiate for Chet's release were fruitless. Deadlines were set and passed. Pleas for his release came from groups throughout the U.S., as well as from Colombia's Minister of Government, German Zea Hernandez, and a Colombian Catholic priest, Garcia Herraros. Herraros's plea is particularly noteworthy:

> We want to ask the kidnappers to free this man who has dedicated his life to the extremely noble task of translating the Bible into an Indian language. We can't become insensitive or indifferent to the pain of our Protestant brothers. We esteem and respect them. We appreciate their efforts of sharing the love of Christ. . . .[2]

The end came on March 7, 1981. Apparently drugged several hours earlier, Chet was taken by his captors in a hijacked minibus and driven around the city for several hours. Then they pulled over and shot Chet once in the heart and fled in a getaway car.

Chet's death came as a shock, but the love of God in the hearts of Chet's wife and parents was so great that the tragedy was viewed in the perspective of God's perfect and sovereign will. Chet's wife remarked, "We committed him to the Lord a long time ago. . . . We have perfect peace."[3] Chet's mother, Mary Bitterman, said after she learned of Chet's death, "Lives have already been changed, so who knows what might happen now because of Chet's death."[4] Chet's father said on the day that his son's body was found, "We have assurance that God planned all this before Chet was born."[5]

Certainly only those who experience an in-love relationship with their heavenly Father could respond in such ways. Chet's deep love relationship with God was also evident to all who knew him. Five years before his death, Chet wrote about his relationship with God on the application for service with Wycliffe:

> Every day I spend approximately one hour alone with God. I approach it as a "date" with God (without meaning to appear sacrilegious). I talk with Him and tell Him what's on my mind, my problems, etc. But I don't want to be a bore and do all the talking on my "date," so then I listen to what He has to say as I read His Word.[6]

In his last days, Chet most assuredly shared his love for and faith in God with his captors, for they complied with his request for a Spanish Bible. A taped message from Chet delivered to a radio station confirmed the fact that he had established a speaking relationship with them. No doubt their conversations much of the time centered around the Lord.

Just two days before his kidnapping in a conversation with his wife, Chet said, "It's okay for someone to die for the sake of getting the Word of God to the minority people of Colombia."[7] Only a man who knows and understands the love of God could make such a statement.

Chet's life and death were a trophy of God's indwelling love, a love that caused him to reciprocate his love by the only model he knew: Christ's supreme example. His love relationship with his Lord was like that of the psalmist, who declared:

> Whom have I in heaven but Thee?
> And besides Thee, I desire nothing on earth.
> My flesh and my heart may fail;
> But God is the strength of my heart and my portion
>   forever.
> For, behold, those who are far from Thee will perish;
> Thou hast destroyed all those who are unfaithful to
>   Thee.
> But as for me, the nearness of God is my good;
> I have made the Lord GOD my refuge.
> That I may tell of all Thy works. (Psalm 73:25-28)

As we look at these three men—Noah, Stephen, and Chet Bitterman—it becomes apparent that having a love relationship with God costs us something. Just as falling in love with another person costs us in time, finances, commitments, and even friends, falling in love with God costs us in effort, time, commitments, worldly involvements, and perhaps even death. It certainly costs us death to ourselves. Just after our Lord instructed the disciples that a man must love Him supremely over and above his own family, He told them to count the costs of following Him, because loving Him supremely meant dying to self:

> "He who does not take his cross and follow after Me is not worthy of Me. He who has found his life shall lose it, and he who has lost his life for My sake shall find it." (Matthew 10:38-39)

The key to Jesus' instruction is that the individual who puts the things of God ahead of his own personal interests will discover true life and love as he has never known it before.

So why develop a love relationship with the Lord? Because not only will we experience and understand God's supreme love enabling us to see things from His perspective, but also we will be intrinsically motivated toward a much higher degree of trust and loyalty. Our ability to move forward and press on for the Lord will not be based on circumstances but on a heart response to our loving heavenly Father.

Nicholas Herman, a soldier and footman in France in the seventeenth century, became a member of the barefooted Carmelites and became known as Brother Lawrence. Brother Lawrence knew what it meant to press on in the love of God. He discovered the reality and joy of a deep, intimate love relationship with the Lord:

> I engaged in a religious life only for the love of God, and I have endeavored to act only for Him; whatever becomes of me, whether I be lost or saved, I will always continue to act purely for the love of God. I shall have this good at least, that till death I shall have done all that is in me to love Him.[8]

NOTES:
1. Betty Blair and Phil Landrum, "Chet Bitterman—Kidnappers' Choice," *In Other Words*, Volume 7, Number 4 (April 1981), page 2.
2. Ruth A. Tucker, *From Jerusalem to Irian Jaya* (Grand Rapids: 1983), page 435.
3. Harry Waterhouse, "We Gave Our Son to God," *In Other Words*, Volume 7 (April 1981), page 4.
4. Waterhouse, *In Other Words*, page 4.
5. Waterhouse, *In Other Words*, page 4.
6. Hugh Steven, "Who Was Chet Bitterman?" *In Other Words*, Volume 7, Number 4 (April 1981), page 5.
7. Steven, *In Other Words*, page 5.
8. Brother Lawrence, *The Practice of the Presence of God* (Old Tappan: Fleming H. Revell, 1981), pages 14-15.

CHAPTER THREE

Examining Your Love

*There is only one kind of love, but
there are a thousand imitations.*
FRANCOIS DE LA
ROCHEFOUCAULD

Examining your love for the Lord is a personal responsibility. No one else could describe the depth of your love for God, nor its quality and intensity. It must be a personal evaluation between you and the Lord, an evaluation based on the understanding that "God sees not as man sees, for man looks at the outward appearance, but the LORD looks at the heart" (1 Samuel 16:7). We must sincerely examine our love for God without any outside influence or bias. We must look beyond what we say or do, and evaluate our true intentions. Based on the results of our findings, we can then establish a plan for what we must do or what changes we need to make in order to experience a deep love relationship with God.

To help illustrate the importance of examination and evaluation, let us consider the conditions for flying a plane. Several of my friends are pilots. Every now and then, I get a call from one asking if I would like to go up and fly for an hour or two. Planes and flying have fascinated me since I was a young boy, so, if I have some time, I usually jump at the offer.

I am continually impressed by each pilot's careful attention to detail. From the moment we arrive at the plane until we land and tie the plane down, the procedure of methodical checks to ensure the safety of the flight is impressively thorough. Every little detail of the plane, the weather conditions, the air traffic, and so on, is observed. Each pilot has been trained to always consider safety first.

I am also amazed at the amount of preparation and training a pilot must undergo. The training never really ends. Evaluations and examinations for all pilots are frequent. After being licensed, a pilot must make a certain number of take-offs and landings in a given period in order to "stay current." Night flying also requires regular training time. Also, a pilot must be "checked out" with each different type of plane before he is authorized to fly it. From physical examinations to evaluations of flying ability, a pilot undergoes extensive monitoring on an ongoing basis for as long as he continues to fly.

The point of having such rigorous standards for pilots should be obvious. Among other things, a pilot must be continually motivated to maintain and improve his flying skills. His physical and mental ability to fly must be kept in top shape. A pilot must not allow the passing of time to cause him to forget all his preparation and training.

In terms of our relationship with God, imagine how many more spiritually mature Christians would be ministering today if we could personally apply these same standards. Regular examinations and evaluations of our Christian life could greatly influence us to grow in the Lord. For example, imagine every member of a church being asked to memorize a certain number of Bible verses every three months and then to be evaluated on his ability to recall those verses. Or perhaps each church member could take a test to find out how much he remembers from the six previous Sunday morning messages and how he has applied them to his life.

These suggestions may seem farfetched, but the idea of personal examination and evaluation of our spiritual life is very important. Perhaps one of the greatest dangers to a believer is the subtle drifting from the Lord in daily Christian life. Because of this possibility, every believer should consider personally examining and evaluating his walk before God frequently, perhaps two to three times a year. As with pilots, a sincere evaluation of our spiritual condition will force us to stay sharp and improve, especially if we enlist the help of another believer for us to be accountable to. Also, these evaluations will indicate to us our rate of maturity, giving us direction for adjustment and change.

But how do we examine and evaluate our love for God? Well, we must be honest with ourselves and ask the Lord for insight into our lives. We must search our hearts and sincerely evaluate the true nature of our love in light of the biblical principles for loving God. Only then will we be able to understand what He expects in our love toward Him, for we will be viewing our love as He views it. Therefore, an honest evaluation of our life and our love for God is our responsibility if we want to develop a true love relationship with Him.

Testing and examining one's life, as well as evaluating one's relationship with God, are alluded to several times in the Bible. In the Old Testament, there is the story about God testing Abraham to give him the opportunity to prove his love and faithfulness to Him. God asked Abraham to sacrifice his beloved son, Isaac. Without hesitating, Abraham proceeded to carry out the Lord's command, only to be stopped at the last moment by an angel of the Lord. God then acknowledged Abraham's love and faithfulness by providing a ram to be sacrificed in place of his son.

There are several instances of God testing Moses and the nation of Israel, from their departure from Egypt to their arrival in the Promised Land (Exodus 15:25, 16:4, 20:20; Deuteronomy 8:2,16; Judges 2:22). These tests were obviously not needed to enlighten God about the spiritual condition of the people. He already knew their hearts. Rather, they served as indicators of faith to Moses and Israel in order to intermittently show them what God expected in their love and loyalty to Him.

Jonah reevaluated his love and loyalty to God while in the stomach of the great fish. While in that dark, living cave, he prayed, "'I have been expelled from Thy sight.' Nevertheless I will look again toward Thy holy temple. . . . But I will sacrifice to Thee with the voice of thanksgiving. That which I have vowed I will pay. Salvation is from the LORD" (Jonah 2:4,9).

In New Testament times, the apostles, as well as many other believers, stood up for the gospel in the face of almost certain death. Why? Because of their love and loyalty to Jesus Christ. James reminded the believers that such tests and trials were intended to produce endurance (James 1:2-4). Therefore, their loyalty to God amid these trials served as a trophy of great love and sacrifice.

In the New Testament, there are two different Greek words for testing by personal examination: *peirazō* and *dokimazō*. As we consider our own love for God, it is important to distinguish between these two words.

Paul, writing to the church at Corinth, challenged the people there, "Test yourselves to see if you are in the faith; examine yourselves! Or do you not recognize this about yourselves, that Jesus Christ is in you—unless indeed you fail the test?" (2 Corinthians 13:5). The Greek word for "examine" in this verse is *peirazō,* which means "to try or to test intentionally, and with the purpose of discovering what good or evil, what power or weakness, was in a person or thing."[1] In this context, members of the Corinthian church were challenged to examine themselves to see whether or not they were true believers.

In 1 Corinthians 11:28, the word *dokimazō* is used for "examine." Here Paul is describing for us the Last Supper, including the requirements for participation. To discourage a person from partaking in an unworthy manner, Paul says, "Let a man examine himself, and so let him eat of the bread and drink of the cup." In this verse, "examine" (*dokimazō*) refers to the "act of testing someone or something for the purpose of approving it."[2] Thus, when a believer has examined his life and has found no sin between him and the Lord for which he has not sought forgiveness, he may partake of the Lord's Table, having approved himself before God.

Thus, there are two different types of testing or examining of oneself: a person examining himself to determine whether or not he is a true believer, and a believer examining his walk before God to determine his worthiness to partake of the Lord's Supper.

Regarding the first type of examination (*peirazō*), a person who does not know for a fact that he is a believer should spiritually settle the matter. But a person who claims to be a Christian but whose life is not in accord with the things of God must also be challenged with this type of personal examination. Many individuals who refer to themselves as Christians do not have an understanding of what a Christian really is, nor do they even know how a person becomes a true believer. In desiring a love relationship with the Lord, such an examination becomes vitally important, for a person cannot truly love God until he has first received His love through salvation. Hence, being a true believer is a condition for truly loving the Lord.

Have you experienced salvation and peace with God? It doesn't just result from attending a church service or Bible study. It must be an act of your will as you humble yourself before God and admit that you are a lost sinner (Romans 3:23). You must believe that Jesus Christ is Lord (Romans 10:9) and that He shed His blood for the pardoning of all your sins. Also, you need to believe that the free gift of eternal life is in Jesus alone (John 14:6, Romans 6:23, Hebrews 9:22). You must then ask Him to take control of your life and receive Him as your Lord and Savior (John 1:12, Romans 10:9-10, Revelation 3:20).

If you sincerely follow these steps, salvation and peace with God will not be a "Maybe" or "I think so." It will be a confident knowledge of a spiritual fact. The apostle John stated, "These things I have written to you who believe in the name of the Son of God, in order that you may know that you have eternal life" (1 John 5:13).

The significance of the second examination (*dokimazō*) lies in the fact that loving the Lord and being worthy to partake of the Lord's Supper are related. The most sacred act of worship for the Church is the Communion service: the Lord's Supper. God requires that we participate in this act of worship in a worthy manner, since a holy God cannot have fellowship with unholiness (1 Corinthians 10:21, 2 Corinthians 6:14-7:1, 1 John 1:5-7). Certainly, involving ourselves in the Lord's Table means coming into close fellowship with Him, commemorating His sacrifice for our salvation with honor and reverence. Thus, we must examine ourselves to make sure that our walk is worthy before we attempt to enter into an intimate love relationship with our holy God (Hebrews 10:22, James 4:8).

Only by abiding in God and His Word, adhering to His standards, can we remain worthy before Him and fully experience the freedom of a perfected love relationship with Him. John declared:

> The one who says, "I have come to know Him," and does not keep His commandments, is a liar, and the truth is not in him; but whoever keeps His word, in him the love of God has truly been perfected. By this we know that we are in Him: the one who says he abides in Him ought himself to walk in the same manner as He walked. (1 John 2:4-6)

In summary, the primary step in examining our love for God focuses on our faith (Are you a true believer?) and on our Christian walk (Are you worthy and upright before God?). Our next step is evaluating our love in view of the biblical principles for loving God.

PRINCIPLES FOR LOVING GOD

Scripture presents for us nine principles to consider in our love for God. Four of these principles establish the standards for a true love for God, and the other five principles characterize the results of a true love. Sincerely consider each principle, applying it to your life as you examine and evaluate your present love for God.

To truly love God, we must . . .
(1) *Love God completely and totally.* "Love the Lord your

God with all your heart, and with all your soul, and with all your mind, and with all your strength" (Mark 12:30). In response to a scribe's sincere question, "What commandment is the foremost of all?" our Lord quoted this Old Testament verse (Deuteronomy 6:5), calling it the greatest commandment. We must, therefore, begin with this verse, for it clearly states our first responsibility. We are to love God completely and totally—heart, soul, mind, and strength—because He alone is God (Mark 12:29). There cannot be anything else in our life competing with our love for Him.

Because God gives Himself totally in His love to us, He expects us to give ourselves totally in our love to Him. If we desire such a relationship with Him, we must be ready to sacrifice anything or anybody who might disrupt our love for Him. There can be no other love in our lives equal to the love we have for the Father. Such a willingness becomes the most important and powerful commitment we could ever make to God. Out of that commitment will evolve the only true motivation for enduring and growing throughout the Christian life. It is the only motivation that will truly cause us to separate ourselves from the things of this world, allowing us to conform more fully to Jesus Christ. Our strength to endure and spiritually mature results from a pure love relationship and an intimate knowledge of God, not from a heart of pride and vainglory to succeed before man.

The process of maintaining a deep, intimate love for the Lord rather than just a "friendship love" will affect the entire person. The depth of our love will determine our attitude and motivation in everything we do in the Christian life. Loving God completely and totally is His standard for us. In such love alone can we measure how consuming our love for Him is to be.

(2) *Love the Lord more than anything or anyone else.* Jesus said, "He who loves father or mother more than Me is not

worthy of Me; and he who loves son or daughter more than Me is not worthy of Me" (Matthew 10:37). I can remember reading this verse as a new Christian and thinking to myself, "How could I ever love someone I can't feel or see more than I love my own mother or wife?" Even a few years later, after getting married, this verse still bothered me. My love for my wife was more than anything else I knew.

But as I discovered the reality of an in-love relationship with the Lord, the true meaning of this verse came alive to me. In this statement, our Lord was instructing the disciples how deep their love for Him was to be. The only way Jesus could communicate such a strong love was to draw a comparison with something the disciples could relate to: the Jewish family, with father, mother, son, and daughter.

Historically, the average Jewish family was filled with love. We see evidence of this in Joseph's devotion to Mary and other expressions of love within the family (Ecclesiastes 9:9, Song of Solomon, Proverbs 31, and so on). So, in order to describe love to the disciples in a way they could understand, Jesus told His disciples that their love for Him had to be greater than their love for any member of their family. If their love for Him was anything less, they were not worthy to be His disciples. In order to impress upon them the importance of loving Him with such great intensity, He drew on the most powerful symbol of love in that day—the family.

We, too, are called to love the Lord more than we love any member of our family, or anyone or anything else. It must be a love characterized by intense devotion, coupled with zeal to be obedient to His Word. It must be the strongest, most powerful, most motivational love that we could possibly have in our lives, a love with no equal. This is God's standard for the quality and intensity of our love for Him.

(3) *Love not the world.* "Do not love the world, nor the

things in the world. If any one loves the world, the love of the Father is not in him" (1 John 2:15). In order to experience a love relationship with the Father, we must be separated from this world, free from its entanglements and control.

In working with young people for a number of years, I often found that the issue of forsaking the visible world for an invisible God was the most difficult commitment young people have to face. Youth tend to respond out of their feelings. The world, with its pleasurable enticements, certainly appeals to their feelings. John was writing to Christians in his generation who apparently had the same problem. John points out that love for the world negates love for the Father, since the world is an evil system under the control of Satan (1 John 5:19).

In order to be in love with God, we must be controlled by God. There should be no other major influences on our lives, especially those subtle influences originating from the world's system. We must each live a one-master life, totally in submission to His will. This is God's standard of love for us that shows the world we are totally His. The psalmist reflects such a heart in love with the Lord:

> Whom have I in heaven but you?
> And being with you, I desire nothing on earth.
> My flesh and my heart may fail,
> but God is the strength of my heart
> and my portion forever. (Psalm 73:25-26, NIV)

(4) *Hate evil.* "Hate evil, you who love the LORD, who preserves the souls of His godly ones, He delivers them from the hand of the wicked" (Psalm 97:10). Evil can be defined as anything that is not in harmony with God's divine order, both physical and moral. Sin does not con-

form to the moral laws of God; therefore, sin is evil.

From this perspective, if we want to love God, we must hate sin. It has been said that sin is man's declaration of independence against God. *Agapē* love requires an element of dependence. Thus, a dependence on God will result in our despising of sin and evil, allowing us to experience a deeper love for the Father.

Most believers are not worried about doing blatant forms of evil such as murder, rape, or robbery. But for them the problems are the "little" evils, which can be just as devastating. Christians do evil to each other through their gossip, bitterness, and slander. In the name of "religion," they parade their so-called spirituality before the people around them. In the meantime, they judge the churches or pastors in their community as being too much of this, or not enough of that, all the while attempting to justify why they worship God in their own way, in their own time. Blaise Pascal has perhaps rightly observed that "men never do evil so completely and cheerfully as when they do it from religious conviction."[3]

We must remember that in view of the holiness of God, sin is sin, regardless of its size or intensity. The Lord recognizes no distinctions. Therefore, we must also hate those "little" evils, such as gossip, bitterness, and slander. We must hate every attitude that is not in harmony with the nature of the holiness of God. We must separate ourselves from every appearance of evil (1 Thessalonians 5:22). Let us be aware of God's indictment of Judah in His response to the people's sin in Isaiah 1:16: "Wash yourselves, make yourselves clean; remove the evil of your deeds from My sight. Cease to do evil."

Separating ourselves from every form of evil will not only allow us to experience a deeper love for the Lord but also to express to Him our loyalty and sincere willingness to be obedient to His commandments. John rightly declared, "This is the love of God, that we keep His commandments; and His commandments are not burdensome" (1 John 5:3).

Let us now consider five principles that will be evident in our lives if we truly love the Lord. They serve as guidelines in our relationship to God—*if* we are maintaining a love relationship with Him.

If you truly love God, then . . .
(1) *You are keeping His Word.* "Whoever keeps [Christ's] word, in him the love of God has truly been perfected. By this we know that we are in Him" (1 John 2:5).

A young man recently came to me for counseling because he said he was losing his motivation for being a Christian. He was angry because God was not answering his prayers for "more" faith and strength to endure temptation. We decided to meet weekly for the next several weeks.

One day while shopping at a grocery store, I overheard a voice from the next aisle that sounded very much like the young man who had come to me for counseling. It was not a matter of my listening in on his conversation, but rather overhearing him as he was speaking loudly. He was bragging to a friend about sleeping with his girlfriend the previous week while his parents were out of town. He told his friend that the following week his parents were going to be gone again and that his girlfriend was going to be staying with him.

Not wanting to feel like I was secretly eavesdropping, I decided I would walk around to his aisle and say hello. As I turned the corner, he walked around the far corner, not noticing me, though I had enough time to confirm my suspicion that it was the young man with whom I was counseling.

Our next meeting was scheduled for three days from

the time of this incident, so I spent a great deal of time in prayer, asking the Lord for wisdom and guidance. I knew that I might be forced to confront him.

In our meeting, we began with prayer and casual talk as usual. He then shared his continual frustration with serving the Lord. He said he was still losing his motivation to be a strong Christian and needed more faith.

I began asking him some personal questions about his life. I asked him if there were things in his life that the Lord would disapprove of. He mentioned telling a lie here and there, and his unwillingness to have devotions on a daily basis. These were the only things he could think of.

We then talked further about sin and its consequences, looking at several Bible verses. We talked about God's extreme displeasure with sin and His great disappointment with us when we choose to dabble in it. Two verses we looked at in particular were Psalm 66:18, which reminds us that sin in our lives will keep God from hearing our prayers, and 1 John 2:6, which tells us that if we say we abide in Him, then we ought to "walk in the same manner as He walked." A heart that has purified itself from sin gives assurance that God hears our prayers (Psalm 66:19, 1 John 3:21), and as we keep His Word and refrain from sin, His love matures in us (1 John 2:5).

I then asked him one more time if he felt there could be anything in his life preventing him from experiencing a closer, more obedient relationship with God. He looked down and was silent for a few moments. He looked back up at me with tears in his eyes. Then he began telling me that over the last couple of months, he and his girlfriend had slipped, having sexual relations and then justifying it by saying they were in love. Now he was admitting before the Lord that it was sin because they were not married.

Together, we got on our knees and he prayed, asking

God's forgiveness. He was finally admitting before God that he had been playing with sin. At last he realized that his sin was the primary factor that had weakened his love for God. This weakening process led to his lack of motivation to endure and grow in the Christian life. But now he finally understood the importance of being obedient to God's commands, thereby allowing God's love to mature and strengthen him.

Desiring to keep God's Word reflects a heart that is maturing in God's love. It is a heart that is controlled by only one master, its dearest loved one, the Lord Jesus Christ (1 John 5:1-3).

(2) *You are known by God and you know God.* "If any one loves God, he is known by Him" (1 Corinthians 8:3). In the book of Galatians, Paul makes it very clear that it is impossible to know God by our own efforts. In fact, in Galatians 4:9, Paul points out that it is God who comes to know us first. He takes the initiative in salvation, and we come to know Him only because we are first known by Him. As a result of becoming Christians, we are now the object of God's personal favor and recognition.

In 1 Corinthians 8:3, Paul used the verb *ginōskō,* which means to know deeply, to know on a personal, intimate level. Therefore, when Paul says that whoever loves God is known by Him, he is saying that the person who truly loves God will experience a close, intimate knowledge of the Father. God imparts knowledge of Himself to us as we mature in our love for Him. Such a relationship ought to manifest itself in our relationship toward our fellowman. John said, "Beloved, let us love one another, for love is from God; and every one who loves is born of God and knows God" (1 John 4:7).

Perhaps this principle is the most important of all, since it becomes visible not only to believers but also to the

world. It is love in action. John declared to us, "Dear children, let us not love with words or tongue but with actions
and in truth" (1 John 3:18, NIV).

(3) *You love the brethren.* "Beloved, if God so loved us, we
also ought to love one another. No one has beheld God at
any time; if we love one another, God abides in us, and His
love is perfected in us" (1 John 4:11-12).

Perhaps at first glance one may conclude without hesitation this third principle from the preceding principle. But
since Scripture has so much to say about love between
Christians—God's love is in fact perfected in us by our love
for our brothers and sisters—this command must stand as a
principle in itself.

As Christians, we must take caution. John warned in
several verses that even though one may claim to know God,
if he does not love his brother (the Christian community),
he is a liar (1 John 4:20). Consequently, he is in spiritual
darkness and walks in that darkness (1 John 2:11). He is
even a murderer (3:15).

On the contrary, everyone who loves his brother will
be known as a disciple of Christ (John 13:34-35), will abide
in the light (1 John 2:10), will have passed from death into
life (3:14), is born of God and knows God (4:7), and will
have God abide in him (4:12).

If we truly love the Lord, then our *agapē* love for other
Christians will be sincere and active. It will be a love that will
never fade away or depend on circumstances. We will love
because He first loved us (1 John 4:19). John could not have
said it more plainly: "This commandment we have from
Him, that the one who loves God should love his brother
also" (1 John 4:21).

(4) *You are not fearing.* "There is no fear in love; but
perfect love casts out fear, because fear involves punishment, and the one who fears is not perfected in love"

(1 John 4:18). One of the special byproducts of God's love is that it frees the believer from fear. Certainly, this experience of spiritual liberation must have been very comforting to the early Christians, who faced almost continual persecution for their faith.

In this verse, John was referring to God's perfect love, not our love for Him, since we are imperfect. But God's perfect love will drive out fear in the believer who has drawn near to Him. The natural byproducts of love are trust and security, which automatically eliminate fear. So, the more we know and love the Lord, the more His perfect love manifests itself in our lives by liberating us from fear. Kenneth Wuest asserts:

> This perfect love is God's love for us, not our love for Him, which later is always most imperfect. To realize that God loves His own with a perfect love, is to know assuredly that He will in His love for us not allow anything to come to us that would work us harm, and that whatever comes of pain or sorrow, of loss or cross, is only for our good.[4]

A believer who is in love with the Lord is secure in his position with Him. He entrusts his life daily to the Lord and knows that whatever occurs is for the best since he is a part of God's perfect plan and perfect love. Is this not Paul's teaching in Romans 8:28? "We know that God causes all things to work together for good to those who love God, to those who are called according to His purpose."

Unquestionably, a mark of an in-love relationship with the Lord is a life free from fear and torment; a life trusting totally in God's perfect love. "By this, love is perfected with us, that we may have confidence in the day of judgment; because as He is, so also are we in this world" (1 John 4:17).

(5) *You are abiding in God.* "We have come to know and have believed the love which God has for us. God is love, and the one who abides in love abides in God, and God abides in him" (1 John 4:16).

In John 15, we read what has been referred to as the Farewell Discourse. Here Jesus dealt with three different relationships that involved the disciples: their relationship with Him, their relationship with each other, and their relationship with the world.

The Lord chose to instruct the disciples about their relationship with Him by telling them the vine metaphor. The disciples would have known a lot about vines because viticulture was common in Israel. To point out the importance of being dependent on Him, the Lord stressed, "Abide in Me, and I in you. As the branch cannot bear fruit of itself, unless it abides in the vine, so neither can you, unless you abide in Me" (John 15:4). The Lord was saying that apart from Him, the disciples could do nothing. His life had to be flowing through their lives in order for them to bear fruit.

Such a relationship cannot be just a casual connection, but it must be a firmly attached bond grafted tightly together. Then and only then can the branch draw the necessary nutrients to grow healthy, productive fruit. John later refers to this bonding in 1 John, relating it to the love of God. He presents his conclusions in a logical sequence: Since God is love, if we abide in love, we abide in God. Hence, if a believer is in love with the Lord, he is also abiding in Him (1 John 4:6).

The key to understanding the importance of this sequence of truths is the verb "abide." The believer who is serious about his love relationship with the Lord understands that abiding in God is far more than just a casual prayer three or four times a week. It is a constant dependence relationship in which he acknowledges the Lord in his daily routine and makes God his first and foremost priority in every area of his life. It is the attitude of a servant who is loyal and content through every circumstance of his life. At the foundation of this relationship is a love the world cannot understand.

Abiding in the Lord is the most peaceful, content, and secure position a believer could ever experience. It was the position in which Paul, who loved the Lord with all his heart, soul, mind, and strength, could stand on a ship in the middle of a violent storm and encourage his own captors, "Keep up your courage, men, for I believe God, that it will turn out exactly as I have been told" (Acts 27:25). Abiding in Christ is having a love relationship with the Lord. The two go hand in hand.

As we consider these principles for loving God, we should gain a better understanding of what God expects in our love for Him. Also, we should be more aware of what we need to do spiritually to place ourselves in position for a love relationship with God.

Let us now move on to application: how to fall in love with the Lord.

NOTES:
1. Kenneth S. Wuest, *Word Studies in the Greek New Testament*, Volume 3 (Grand Rapids: Eerdmans, 1974), page 127.
2. Wuest, *Word Studies*, Volume 3, page 126.
3. Frank S. Mead, ed., *Encyclopedia of Religious Quotations* (Old Tappan: Fleming H. Revell, 1965), page 127.
4. Wuest, *Word Studies*, Volume 3, page 72.

CHAPTER FOUR

The Love Relationship

We are shaped and fashioned by
what we love.
JOHANN WOLFGANG
VON GOETHE

One of the more pleasing duties of being a pastor is performing the wedding service. Uniting two people before God in the presence of witnesses always gives me a thrill. But perhaps what I enjoy the most is not so much the service but rather the premarital counseling preceding the service. Usually I like to spend seven sessions with a couple: six sessions before the wedding, and one session three months after the wedding.

In the second session I usually discuss with the couple their love relationship. I ask them to describe their love for each other and why they love each other. They write out their answers on paper without any discussion with their partner. Over the years I have heard some very interesting descriptions of love and reasons for love. "My love for Gary makes me think." "I love Betty because she is strong and healthy." My personal favorite is, "I love Jim because my mother likes the kinds of clothes he wears."

But usually the couples I work with have a very strong and biblically healthy description of their love. They understand the sacrifice and commitment. They recognize the importance of trust and loyalty. Furthermore, the excitement and vitality of their love for each other is unmistakably transparent.

Recently a young lady was married in our church. As a single lady, Linda had always been very active in our church. She had a real heart for service. One day, she met Brett. Within a couple of months, she began to change. Little things did not seem to bother her much any more. She exhibited a greater tolerance for people and manifested a genuine excitement for God and life. People who knew her well dismissed any comments about her change in character by saying, "Oh, she's in love!"

The love she had for Brett had taken control of her. The joy and excitement of her love relationship changed her entire approach to life and its difficulties. Her attitude was one of youthful enthusiasm and delight.

CHARACTERISTICS

What about a love relationship with the Lord? Should it have the same characteristics as that of a newly engaged or married couple? Should it be marked by a fresh excitement and enthusiasm that is obvious through actions and conversation? Should it be a love that motivates a believer continually in an attitude of optimism and delight?

The answer is unequivocally *yes!* For what greater friend and lover could we have than our Maker, who is indeed "the Rock"? "His work is perfect, for all His ways are just; a God of faithfulness and without injustice, righteous and upright is He" (Deuteronomy 32:4).

Our love relationship with God is not a momentary emotional experience, but rather a disciplined act of our will, founded on a deep reverence and submission to a holy and loving God. Such a kinship is the most powerful and dynamic relationship we could ever experience. It is an invincible association with God, who is Himself *love*. His love cannot be matched by any earthly relationship or experience, for there is no greater expression of love than His sacrifice of His only Son for the remission of our sins (John 15:3, Hebrews 9:22, 1 John 3:16).

In order to provide us a glimpse of His intimate love and to give us a recognizable pattern to show us what He desires in a love relationship, He has given us some biblical examples to observe.

The Old Testament writers often described the love relationship between God and the Israelites as that of a loving husband wanting to bring back his erring wife from her troubled ways. On several occasions, Moses reminded the people of God's intimate love for them despite their failures: "Yet on your fathers did the LORD set His affection to love them . . . even you above all peoples, as it is this day" (Deuteronomy 10:15; see also Deuteronomy 4:37, 7:7-8, 33:3).

In the New Testament, the marriage bond between two believers is related to Christ's love for the Church:

> For this cause a man shall leave his father and mother, and shall cleave to his wife; and the two shall become one flesh. This mystery is great; but I am speaking with reference to Christ and the church. (Ephesians 5:31-32)

In this passage Paul quoted Genesis 2:24, which is the most profound and basic statement in the entire Bible concerning God's design for marriage. Interestingly, this verse is directly after the reference to Adam recognizing that Eve was a part of himself. It is this kind of intimacy within the marriage bond that the Lord refers to as unique, holy, and undefiled. Therefore, it is the highest form of every human relationship known to man. It also becomes an example to us of the character of our love for the Lord.

Our love relationship with God should be reflected in a marriage bond that is unique, holy, and inviolable. Marriage is a relationship that provoked theologian Charles Williams to write that he was "startled to find romantic love an exact correlation and parallel of Christianity."[1] The characteristics of a deep, intimate love within Christian marriage serve as a pattern for our love for God.

In Ephesians 5:32, Paul relates the marriage bond to Christ's love for the Church, concluding that the actual bond (cleaving and becoming one flesh) is a mystery, which is also likened to Christ (the Bridegroom) joining to His Bride (the Church). A. Skevington Wood stated, "Genesis 2:24 enunciates a more profound truth than was realized till Christ came to win His Bride, the Church, by giving Himself for her on the cross (verse 25)."[2] Ed Wheat alluded to the love relationship in the Christian marriage as emblematic of Christ's relationship to His Church:

> This reminds us that true romantic love, undergirded by *agapē* and enjoyed in the permanent context of Christian marriage, beautifully portrays the love relationship of Jesus Christ and His church.[3]

What better examples of intimate love are there for us to observe than Christ's supreme love for His Church and the love within Christian marriage? The Lord designed and established both of them—for His delight and our joy. Therefore, our response in love to the Lord should reflect His examples to us, and should be nothing short of our complete and total commitment—free from any conditions or restrictions.

May our love for God be filled with delight, joy, excitement, and anticipation. May it be sincere and intimate so as to keep us in perfect peace. May it be fresh and creative, always searching for new ways to express our heart in love to the God of love. For He delights in those who place their hope in His love. "The LORD delights in those who fear him, who put their hope in his unfailing love" (Psalm 147:11, NIV).

PREPARING FOR THE LOVE RELATIONSHIP
Properly preparing oneself for a love relationship with the Lord cannot be overlooked or overemphasized. Preparing yourself to draw near to a holy God will require:

- Your *decision* to fully commit yourself to pursue a love relationship with God. This decision is made after your personal examination of your life and your spiritual condition.

- Your *commitment* to cast off the influences of the world and the desires of the flesh, which are not in agreement with the Lord's commandments nor honoring to His glory.

- Your *understanding* of three very important aspects involved in the love relationship: your approach to the Lord, your ability to give time and effort, and your willingness to be tested. Each of these aspects must be thoroughly understood and accepted before your love relationship can achieve the depth that will truly make an impact in your life.

(1) *The decision*—If, after you have sincerely examined yourself, you find that your present love for God is short of what He desires (based on the principles listed in Chapter 3), then you need to decide to make the changes and adjustments necessary for a true love relationship with the Lord. This decision must be sincere and genuine, for it must be strong enough to endure the pains of change and perhaps even persecution. It is at this point that a believer who is serious about knowing and loving God and a believer who wants to be more "spiritual" will separate. Wanting to be more "spiritual" can earn recognition from man. But it often becomes self-seeking, because such a believer tends to give glory not to God but to himself. Then when the difficult times come, he lacks the strength to endure. We must all be willing to stand firm. Do not make the decision to commit yourself to change if you are not willing to count the cost.

(2) *The commitment*—Making the decision to fall in love with the Lord is one thing. The commitment to follow through with the work of casting off the ungodly influences of the world and flesh is another. As you voluntarily separate yourself from those things that do not bring honor and glory to the Lord, your love for Him will grow in depth and intensity.

The Bible has much to say about ridding ourselves of ungodly influences (Romans 12:1-2, Galatians 5:16, Ephesians 4:21-24). An interesting term describing this casting off process has been provided by theologians: "progressive sanctification." As we progressively set ourselves apart from ungodly influences, we grow and mature in the love and knowledge of God.

(3) *The understanding*—You must carefully consider and thoroughly understand three very important aspects of the love relationship. One involves our approach to the relationship, and the other two involve the relationship itself.

First, you must not flippantly approach God in prayer, boldly announcing that you intend to establish a love relationship with Him. This may be the mind-set of an individual whose real purpose for such a relationship is not for the honor and glory of God but for a self-serving, pious spirituality. The love relationship is not so much to be pursued to make us more spiritual, but rather to honor and glorify Almighty God through our devotion, worship, adoration, and obedience. It must come from a humble heart that is only concerned with delighting the Father. It must evolve out of a heart that aspires to obey His commandments.

Thus, your prayer to God should be clothed in humility as you seek His wisdom and leading. You must commit yourself totally to Him, verbalizing your sincere and genuine desire to *know* Him well.

Second, you must understand that a love relationship does not happen overnight, but over time. How much time? That depends on your level of spiritual maturity and willingness to count the cost. These go hand in hand. The greater your spiritual maturity (seeing and understanding things from God's perspective), the greater your ability to accept the sacrifices you must make to draw near to God and to continue in His work.

You must be aware that such a relationship with God may cost you your best friend, or your social status, or even your job. Why? Because one of those areas of your life may be subtly influencing you away from God, preventing you from truly experiencing the deepest love relationship possible. A relationship with the Lord will definitely cost you in time and effort, just as it takes time and effort for a love relationship to develop between two people. What kind of love could ever develop between two people who never spend time with each other, or who never put forth an effort to give sacrificially to each other? Likewise, a love relationship with God requires time and effort: time to examine and prepare yourself, sacrificing those things that may be pleasing in the flesh but contrary to God; effort to firmly establish and faithfully maintain the love relationship in your life.

Examining, preparing, and finally establishing my love relationship with God took a number of months. It meant giving up some things that previously seemed quite acceptable and important. As long as those things were in my life, the Lord was not my only controlling master. Once I made the decision to fully commit myself to developing a love relationship, the choice to give up those things was not hard. The importance of truly loving God and being obedient to Him was my only goal.

For most believers, the most difficult factor in the love relationship is time. The commitment to spend time with the Lord means we have less time to do the things we are currently doing. For the most part, we must be honest with ourselves and admit that the majority of our time is for our own good and pleasure. We all need to understand that spending time with the Lord is a unique source of joy and contentment, one that could never be equaled by any earthly enjoyment.

Third, you must be ready and willing to accept the probability that your new love relationship with God may be tested by the Lord Himself. In Deuteronomy 13, the Israelites were instructed how to discern a false prophet. The Lord declared that He was testing their love for Him:

"If a prophet or a dreamer of dreams arises among
you and gives you a sign or a wonder, and the sign or
the wonder comes true, concerning which he spoke to
you, saying, 'Let us go after other gods (whom you
have not known) and let us serve them,' you shall not
listen to the words of that prophet or that dreamer of
dreams; for the LORD your God is testing you to find
out if you love the LORD your God with all your heart
and with all your soul. You shall follow the LORD your
God and fear Him; and you shall keep His commandments, listen to His voice, serve Him, and cling
to Him." (Deuteronomy 13:1-4)

This is indeed a significant passage, for it reveals to us God's
great desire to confirm our true love to Him. It also warns us
not to allow ourselves to be led by our feelings or emotions
without head knowledge. A genuine response of the heart,
the seat of our emotions, must first be rooted in the fact of
our faith in God, which results from an acknowledgment of
His truth (the Bible) and His reality (His existence). When
we take this kind of genuine approach, we become discerning enough to protect ourselves from those preachers or
prophets who speak in a profound manner but are out of
line with the Word of God.

This passage is also a reminder to all of us that if we
develop a love relationship with God, He may choose to test
how genuine our love is. There are certainly many biblical
figures who encountered such tests: Adam, Abraham,
Moses, Esther, Job, Daniel, Paul, and John, to name only a
few. I have also heard many people directly relate how God
tested their love for Him soon after they made a commitment toward a closer relationship with Him.

I recall an especially trying situation in my own life
where the Lord clearly tested my love for Him. It was one of

the most difficult times of spiritual and emotional endurance I have ever experienced.

* * *

It had been a little over a year since I had begun to develop a deep, intimate relationship with the Lord. My love relationship with God made me profoundly aware of His presence, which motivated me to want to know Him deeper and deeper.

Abruptly and without warning, I was without a job, and I stayed that way for the next nine months. Not doing the thing I love so much—the work and service of the ministry—made it especially painful. At first, I questioned the Lord for allowing such a thing to occur. After all, I was not guilty of breaking any moral or ethical law, and it had been a whole year and a half since I had put my life back together with the Lord and my wife. I had been serving Him faithfully all that time. So why did a God of love permit me to be cut off and subjected to tremendous periods of loneliness, fear, and emotional and spiritual depression?

The answer came quite clearly to me one day while I was alone, cutting wood high in the Sawtooth Mountains: God was testing my love for Him! I had to prove that my love for Him was not based on my position, salary, or my lot in life. With the exception of my marriage, He stripped me of everything I had found security in, so that if I was truly in love with Him, I would rely only on my relationship with Him for strength and endurance.

Those remaining months for my wife and me became one of the more spiritually exciting periods in our lives. God was revealing to me more and more of His character through my faithfulness during a time when my future was totally uncertain. That was His point in testing me. God was strengthening my love relationship with Him through my total dependence on Him. He was also building up my spiritual character for the work ahead:

> And not only this, but we also exult in our tribulations; knowing that tribulation brings about perseverance; and perseverance, proven character; and proven character, hope; and hope does not disappoint; because the love of God has been poured out within our hearts through the Holy Spirit who was given to us. (Romans 5:3-5)

A very special verse served to minister to me during those difficult days. It is a verse all of us should carry around in our pockets for daily reference. It is the last part of Nehemiah 8:10: ". . . for the joy of the LORD is your strength." My love relationship with the Lord created a supernatural joy. It was a kind of joy not based on circumstance, but rather based on the reality of God's intimate presence in my life. Thus, trusting totally in the One I loved, I could say with Paul in all confidence, "I have learned to be content in whatever circumstance I am" (Philippians 4:11).

Even today, I am very conscious of my joy in the Lord because it is directly related to my love for God. Consequently, if my love weakens, my strength to endure weakens. But throughout my difficult time, because my love for God was deep, I never entertained the idea of quitting. We must not forget that our love for God provides the true joy in life.

* * *

Take some time to seriously consider each of these aspects of the love relationship: your attitude in prayer, the time commitment, and the possibility of being tested. Make sure you understand them and accept their conclusions. After you have examined your life before God and are willing to make the decision to pursue Him in a love relationship, committing yourself to remove anything in your life that may be a hindrance, then *move* to establish the greatest intimate relationship available to man: a true in-love relationship with Almighty God! Heed the encouragement of the author of the book of Hebrews:

> Let us draw near to God with a sincere heart in full assurance of faith, having our hearts sprinkled to cleanse us from a guilty conscience and having our bodies washed with pure water. Let us hold unswervingly to the hope we profess, for he who promised is faithful. (Hebrews 10:22-33, NIV)

ESTABLISHING THE LOVE RELATIONSHIP
So how do we begin to draw near to God in a love relationship? Before we consider the manner, let us first be cautioned about some danger areas in our reverence to Him.

Isaiah records for us a very startling passage in which the Lord is responding angrily to the people of Israel:

> Then the Lord said, "Because this people draw near with their words and honor Me with their lip service, but they remove their hearts far from Me, and their reverence for Me consists of tradition learned by rote, therefore behold, I will once again deal marvelously with this people, wondrously marvelous; and the wisdom of their wise men shall perish, and the discernment of their discerning men shall be concealed." (Isaiah 29:13-14)

There are two very important don'ts listed in this passage. First, we are told not to merely revere God with lip service.

What we say to Him with our words must be complemented and backed up by what we do. In other words, if we tell the Lord that we "praise" Him and "glorify" Him, then we had better praise Him outside of our prayer life and glorify Him through our actions. Many times I have heard people say honoring words in prayer to God, yet their lives do not match what they're saying because they are not truly living what they say they feel. They thank God for His "wonderful faithfulness," yet they live in fear and anxiety of the future. What they are doing is showing false respect: a respect that looks good to man but is clearly disrespectful to God. When we revere God (as Jesus instructs us regarding prayer in Matthew 6:5-13), we are acknowledging His greatness and holiness. Therefore, let us truly live in response to His greatness and holiness. Our words to Him must come from a thankful and loving heart that does not need to "put on" before man.

Second, we must not come to the Lord simply by way of a daily routine. Our devotions with Him are not to turn into a mechanical obligation that exists purely to keep us from feeling guilty for not spending time with Him. This was one of the reasons for God's anger toward the Israelites: because their reverence for Him consisted of "tradition learned by rote." Rather, our time with the Lord must be daily, it is true, but not a rote, habitual, boring routine that is approached the same way every day. The Lord cherishes creative and spontaneous expressions of love toward Him. He loves it when we feel the freedom to just stop whatever we are doing and express our adoration to Him.

I know a young man who used to think of some of the most creative ways to express his love to God. On a Saturday, he might pack some food and drive alone to a quiet place in the mountains. He would then construct a little altar out of stone to the Lord and build a fire, representing the sacrifice of his life to the Lord. Or on a weekday he might take a notebook and go to the nearest stream, away from any distractions, and write out twenty-six reasons why he loved the Lord, using the letters A through Z.

Ideas for expressing our love and devotion to God are limited only by our imagination. Our time of devotion to God should be special, just as a man in love with his new bride creatively shares his love with her.

Now, do not misunderstand. I am not criticizing the "daily devotional." But we have confused the daily devotional with personal Bible study. For many of us, we sit down, perhaps even daily, and spend five to ten minutes reading the Bible. Then we pray for a few minutes, asking God for this and for that, treating Him like a spiritual Santa Claus, and we call this our daily devotions. We have missed the point! Devotions, in the truest sense, are not for *us*. They are for God! The reason for our daily devotions to Him are not so much to keep us strong, but rather to please God. Through our devotions, we honor Him as King of kings, worshiping Him in His greatness and holiness, giving Him the love and adoration He deserves.

Personal daily Bible study is for our instruction and spiritual growth in the knowledge of the Lord and His Word. It is for helping us mature in the faith. Devotions, though they are an encouragement to us, are primarily for God's enjoyment. Our devotional life and our personal Bible study must be viewed separately, for each has its distinctive purpose. But both must be an active part in our love relationship with the Lord. More about this later in the chapter.

* * *

As we view how to establish and maintain a love relationship with God, let us consider Christ's example. He resolutely pursued His close, intimate fellowship with the Father on a regular basis.

At least six different occasions are recorded in the Gospels where Jesus goes up to a mountain (sometimes referred to as the wilderness) alone to pray and spend time with God. In fact, Luke 5:16 mentions that Jesus would often slip away in the wilderness to pray, suggesting that it was a repeated action. Why would Jesus have to slip away? Because He chose to be alone. He chose to spend great amounts of time with the Father, separated from all distractions. It was during these times that Jesus would commune with God in deep, intimate prayer, drawing near to Him.

Jesus' example is the key to the depth of our love relationship with God. There is no better way to grow in our love than to spend time alone with God. The intimacy and closeness with the Lord from a time of prayer and meditation—free from all distractions—cannot be matched in any other way.

In my own life, my time alone with the Lord is vital both to my spiritual and emotional life, as well as to my ministry. Living at the foot of the Rocky Mountains provides me with a number of special places to go to for an hour or two. One in particular is well away from the noise of the highway, situated at the crest of a twenty-foot waterfall. At times, I have spent up to six hours there with the Lord, praying, rejoicing in His love, and memorizing verses from the Psalms. Not only do these times draw me closer to Him, but they also free me from the mental and emotional strains of daily living, thus allowing me to keep in perspective who God is and what my walk with Him should be like.

With the importance of spending time alone with God in mind, let us now detail some specific things we should do in establishing and maintaining the love relationship. In order to better clarify these items, I have organized them into two different catagories: *active involvement* (our physical actions—John 3:18) and *passive involvement* (physically inactive, but mentally active—Mark 12:30).

Active involvement activities:
1. Personal devotions and prayer
2. Personal and group Bible study
3. Service and fellowship in the Body of Christ

Passive involvement activities:
1. Submission   (heart)
2. Dying to self   (soul)
3. Humility of spirit   (mind)
4. Willingness   (strength)

ACTIVE INVOLVEMENT

Active physical involvement plays a very important role in our love relationship with God. It displays our willingness to *act* upon the relationship, spending our time and effort.

As I mentioned earlier, our devotions to God and our personal Bible study should be viewed separately. Devotions communicate our adoration, devotion, and worship to God. They can be expressed through our prayers, meditation, song, or simply stated out loud. The Psalms record numerous occasions when David expressed himself to God in devotions through prayer and song. One such passage is Psalms 8:9-9:2:

> O LORD, our Lord, how majestic is Thy name in all the earth! I will give thanks to the LORD with all my heart; I will tell of all Thy wonders. I will be glad and exult in Thee; I will sing praise to Thy name, O Most High.

An active prayer life is foundational to our love relationship with God. Just as Jesus regarded prayer His top priority in

His times alone with the Father, so we must also emphasize prayer in our devotions, Bible study, and service. To pray without ceasing is an attitudinal mind-set in which we live in constant communication with God, both verbal and non-verbal. Whether we are alone, praying at the top of a mountain, or simply driving the car through traffic, our mind-set should be one of prayerful conviction, setting our mind "on the things above, not on the things that are on earth" (Colossians 3:2).

Our active involvement through both personal and group Bible study and our service and fellowship within the Body of Christ must also play a part in establishing and maintaining our love relationship. Our involvement affirms our private worship and study. Unfortunately, many Christians count their service and involvement in the Body of Christ as their only "symbolic" demonstration of their love for God. Because they have limited themselves in time, they can only afford to give time to the Lord through regular activities such as attendance in church services or related church functions. Not that attending church is wrong. No, our assembling together is very important! But my point is that many Christians never become involved personally with the Lord beyond attending church services. Consequently, they never experience the beautiful reality of a close, intimate love relationship with God.

How much time should we allot for our active involvements? Well, this will depend on our level of concentration (our ability to withstand distractions) and our motivation (how much we desire to truly know and love God).

Let me offer some suggestions. The following chart shows major active involvements, a suggested frequency for these involvements, and suggested amounts of time for the activities. The time investment varies, depending on whether we are referring to someone who is beginning to establish a love relationship with the Lord or someone who is maintaining an already established love relationship. Note that the amount of time we spend personally with God should increase as we learn to grow more dependent on the Lord through our love relationship:

Activity	Frequency	Time (Establishing)	Time (Maintaining)
Devotions	Daily	5 minutes	5 minutes
Prayer	Daily	5 minutes	10 minutes
Personal Bible study	Daily	10 minutes	15 minutes
Group Bible study	Weekly	1 hour	1-2 hours
Service (ministry related)	Weekly	1 hour	1-2 hours
Fellowship (church worship service and church functions)	Weekly	2 hours	2-4 hours

Please remember that this chart is merely a suggestion. You may not be able to give this much time or effort, or perhaps you can give more time and effort. Whatever the case, the important factor to keep in mind is *quality*. It is how we use our time, especially alone with God, that counts.

PASSIVE INVOLVEMENT

By "passive involvement" I am not suggesting idleness, but rather our internal activity dealing with our mental, spiritual, and emotional processes. What we do in our active involvements will be based on our internal condition. Thus, it is important that we work on those areas that are basic to our personality and temperament, allowing the Lord to refine and approve us: "Blessed is a man who perseveres under trial; for once he has been approved, he will receive the crown of life, which the Lord has promised to those who love Him" (James 1:12).

Our passive activities of submission, dying to self, humility of spirit, and willingness can be summed up in what Vernon Grounds refers to as the "Gethsemane mind-set."[4] The Garden of Gethsemane was where Jesus Christ was betrayed but also where He displayed tremendous loyalty and commitment in doing the will of the Father over and above His own desire for self-preservation.

How could this be important in our love for God? Because such self-sacrifice involves the total person: the heart, mind, soul, and strength. We are called to invest our whole being in our love for God (Mark 12:30). If we are going to truly devote our time and effort to knowing and loving God, we will need a "Gethsemane mind-set." This means submitting ourselves to God's will through our trustful obedience (submission), surrendering ourselves for the sake of His glory (dying to self), humbling ourselves before His wisdom and power (humility of spirit), and committing ourselves to be used freely as He wishes (willingness).

So, how do we develop a "Gethsemane mind-set"? Well, it certainly does not evolve overnight. To gain such a mind-set, we must do three basic things: (1) We should pray, asking the Lord for insight and wisdom into our character. God alone can show us the areas within us that need work. Also, seek a mature Christian who knows you well, and ask this person to candidly share with you whatever he may have noticed in your character that could be a hindrance in your walk with God and in your relationships with others.

(2) We all need to create opportunities that will allow us to develop in those areas that need work. For example, in my own life, there are times when I have difficulty tolerating proud, opinionated people. This intolerance relates to the area of "dying to self." The reason I become intolerant is that this type of person rubs against my own basic selfish character when I become preoccupied with my *wants* rather than the *needs* of others.

In order to work on this area in my life, I have created several opportunities to practice and work through my attitude. One situation was when I asked to be placed on a certain committee made up of several strong, opinionated people. I knew that serving with such people would help me practice dying to self, which would enable me to become more like Jesus Christ. Creating such opportunities for growth are necessary for our internal spiritual health.

(3) One more helpful step in the process of creating a "Gethsemane mind-set" is to locate a mature believer to become accountable to for the internal changes you need to make. Our willingness to share our weaknesses with a brother or sister for the sake of our spiritual improvement is a sign that we are serious about loving the Lord. The person who is committed to loving the Lord will accept accountability with open arms, knowing that his personal improvement will enhance his love relationship with God.

You may never complete these three suggestions or make them a reality in your life as long you remain here on earth. But the important thing is that you continue working on them so long as God reveals areas in your life that need change. As long as we are in the flesh, there will be areas for improvement.

Brother Lawrence certainly experienced a deep, intimate love relationship with the Lord. Writing to a friend who had just lost one of his own close friends, Brother

Lawrence reminded him of the necessity of experiencing a close relationship with God:

> Pray remember what I have recommended to you, which is, to think often of God, by day, by night, in your business, and even in your diversions. He is always near you and with you; leave Him not alone. You would think it rude to leave a friend alone who came to visit you; why, then, must God be neglected? Do not, then, forget Him, but think on Him often, adore Him continually, live and die with Him; this is the glorious employment of a Christian.[5]

What special words for such a special relationship! In them, we can envision the love relationship: the adoration, devotion, and worship that His greatness demands. Thus, in our love, let us commit our adoration to Him, in awe of His greatness and power, acknowledging Him as the one and only God, Creator of everything. Let us commit our loyalty to Him in humility as we honor His supreme sacrifice on our behalf, recognizing His divine love and grace. Let us commit our worship to Him as we bow down in reverence to His holiness and justice, submitting ourselves to Him by casting our crowns of life before His throne. Let us love Him with all our energy because of who He is: God! Certainly the privilege of drawing near to Him is the greatest opportunity afforded mankind. Let us rejoice in our privilege and take the first steps.

NOTES:
1. Ed Wheat, *Love Life for Every Married Couple* (Grand Rapids: Zondervan, 1980), page 247.
2. Frank E. Gaebelein, ed., *The Expositor's Bible Commentary*, Volume II (Grand Rapids: Zondervan, 1978), page 78.
3. Ed Wheat, *Love Life*, page 95.
4. Vernon Grounds, *Radical Commitment* (Portland: Multnomah, 1984), page 41.
5. Brother Lawrence, *The Practice of the Presence of God*, page 54.

CHAPTER FIVE

Time Alone with God

*God does not ask about our ability
or inability, but our availability.*
THE ARKANSAS BAPTIST

For many of us, the frantic pace of life coupled with the daily routine of work and obligations condition us to greatly value our free time. We plan our weekend activities and vacations well in advance. We are cautious with outside commitments (including church activities) in order to preserve our personal free time. And, what little time we do have to ourselves is many times interrupted by fatigue or sudden minor emergencies.

When we spend time with the Lord reading His Word, many times we end up drifting mentally, thinking about things we have done or things we need to do. Furthermore, because our time is so limited, we do not fully understand or appropriate what we do or read during that time. It is no wonder that one of the major frustrations many Christians experience is the problem of maintaining quality time with the Lord.

In Chapter 4 we looked at the importance of involving ourselves in several activities in order to establish and maintain a love relationship with God. First and foremost of these activities is our personal time with the Lord. Practically speaking, how do we maintain a healthy, consistent pattern for spending quality time with God? What can we do to help us toward a daily period that will glorify Him and bring encouragement to us, without letting it fizzle out or become a wearisome obligation?

There are, of course, no easy steps, no easy answers for maintaining a daily time with the Lord. Living in a society that places so many demands on our time invariably causes the time we set aside to seem like a sacrifice. And, perhaps that is exactly what God wants it to be. He loves to see us freely give ourselves to Him. He really wants us to give up something valuable to us just to be with Him. If we make this sacrifice, then we are loving Him not just in lip service but in deed and truth. Accordingly, our love for Him grows because it is, in one sense, earned. It is a love that has cost us something: our time and effort. Thus, sacrificing our time to spend a few minutes with Him is an expression of our love.

THE NEED

A key principle for maintaining a consistent personal time with the Lord and His Word is our understanding and recognition of the *need* to do so. We must recognize how important it is to our spiritual growth to draw daily on God's strength, wisdom, character, and love. In illustration, consider the marriage relationship. Have you ever observed a marriage grow strong where the couple did not work on their love relationship by expressing their love to each other and sharing intimate emotional moments? A marriage will wither away and die if there are no expressions of love, no means of closeness.

Just as a marriage requires two people to express their love to each other daily, in both words and deeds, our love for God must also be expressed daily for His enjoyment and our encouragement. Our time alone with Him is our means of expressing our love to Him. Our spiritual needs are met by the strength, joy, wisdom, and love we draw from Him. We need to be totally dependent on Him . . . daily!

Though we may be truly in love with God, over a period of time we may drift from our consistent daily time with Him. We miss a day here and there. Soon it's three or four days in a row. Then, before we realize it, we have missed having time with the Lord for a month. It's as if we have tried to be independent of Him.

I often overlook my times with God when things are going great. When everything is working smoothly and I am on the top of all my responsibilities, I have a tendency to forget about spending time with Him. Why? Because there are no pressing needs in my life, no urgent matters to discuss with Him. Consequently, I am not forced to be conscious of my need to be dependent on Him. Thus, I am indirectly exalting myself, only coming to Him in times of need.

Perhaps we can relate this dilemma to Paul's "thorn in the flesh." To keep Paul from exalting himself and to help him stay dependent on Him, God gave him a thorn in the flesh. Here Paul describes the Lord's reasoning:

> Concerning this [thorn in the flesh] I entreated the Lord three times that it might depart from me. And He has said to me, "My grace is sufficient for you, for

power is perfected in weakness." Most gladly, therefore, I will rather boast about my weaknesses, that the
power of Christ may dwell in me. Therefore I am well
content with weaknesses, with insults, with distresses,
with persecutions, with difficulties, for Christ's sake;
for when I am weak, then I am strong. (2 Corinthians
12:8-10)

Paul certainly understood and welcomed the *need* for
dependence on God, for this dependence was his strength.

Unfortunately, sometimes in order to get our attention
if we have drifted from our dependence on Him, God may
choose to jolt us in one way or another. It may be His way of
reminding us to keep our eyes on Him, to be daily dependent on Him.

A friend of mine recently encountered such a reminder.
His experience certainly reemphasized to him the importance of spending quality time with the Lord and constantly
depending on Him. Although my friend will never forget
the pain, he will also never forget the valuable lesson of that
experience.

It was late in the evening when John phoned me. He
was a member of the staff at a nearby church. We held
similar staff positions in our respective churches. As John
spoke, I immediately noticed a very somber tone in his
voice. It was the voice of a depressed and shaken young
man.

As a result of a church inquisition aimed at him earlier
that evening, John was demoralized to the point of resigning his position and quitting the ministry altogether. And he
was calling me in need of support and encouragement.

On the verge of breaking down and crying, John pain-
fully shared with me how he sat before several church
families, listening as they vented their criticisms and con-

cerns about his work and his attitude. Over a three-hour period, he was grilled for supposedly having an arrogant attitude and making several poor decisions. It was their conclusion that he lacked spiritual maturity and a willingness to submit to constructive criticism.

As John continued to relate more of the details, I sensed a certain amount of anger and bitterness building in his feelings toward the families. He was beginning to criticize some of them personally, making issues out of unrelated facts, perhaps to discredit them and their criticisms of him.

Whenever a situation such as this arises, I am filled with mixed emotions. On one hand, I want to remain as objective as possible, giving every possible consideration to the complaints aired. On the other, I want to defend another brother in the ministry who has given a portion of his life to serve the Lord and to meet the needs of others. In John's case, I wanted to defend him but was reluctant to do so as I observed his increasingly bitter attitude.

After a few more minutes, I asked John if we could pray over the phone. After I finished praying, he was silent. He then shared with me that he did not feel like praying.

John was relatively new in the ministry. He had never been involved in such a meeting before. Thus I readily understood why he was talking about quitting the ministry. He felt dejected and unappreciated, with no motivation to endure and see it through. He felt that they weren't giving him a fair chance.

I began to ask him questions about his relationship with God. How was his prayer and devotional life? What had God been teaching him lately? And what, in his opinion, was God doing in this particular situation? As he started to respond, he broke down and cried. After a few moments, he began to share about the lack of time he had been giving solely to the Lord. He said he had not spent any personal time with the Lord for over two months because things at home and at church had been so busy. In fact, about the only time he had prayed during that period was with his family at the dinner table and at a couple of church Bible studies.

Because John had become caught up in the snare of schedules, meetings, and deadlines, he lost sight of his need to depend on the Lord. Instead, he was depending on his own wisdom for doing God's business, not relying on God's strength for endurance. Consequently, his response to the criticism of that evening came from an attitude of personal pride, not from a godly mind-set, which would have better prepared him to accept the criticisms in a constructive manner.

As we talked on the phone, John began to recognize that his negative, emotional response to the meeting that evening stemmed directly from his weak relationship with the Lord. He also surmised that his poor attitude and poor decisions were related to his weakened spiritual condition. And so he resolved that he was going to reestablish his daily time with the Lord. But first he knew that he had to seek God's forgiveness for his attitude and for failing to appreciate those families God had used to bring John back to Him.

A month later, John phoned me to let me know how things were going. He said that everything had worked out with the families who had confronted him and that he was feeling better about his attitude and ministry than ever before. Not that all the daily trials of ministry had ceased! Rather, his renewed intimate walk with the Lord was now giving him the strength and confidence to live as a servant of God and to depend daily on Him for wisdom in shepherding His flock.

John knew all along what it meant to be in love with the Lord, but he gradually drifted from the relationship because he neglected his personal time with God. It is important for us to recognize and learn from John's example. But we also need to consider the individual who is consistent in spending quality time with the Lord yet is encountering many difficult trials.

Does spending quality time daily with God free us from problems or difficult circumstances? No! In fact, many times it works in the opposite direction. For example, let's say that in your quiet time you tell the Lord that you want to know Him more deeply through His faithfulness. What would be the best way for you to gain an understanding of His character through His faithfulness? Studying the Bible? Yes. Talking with your pastor? Yes. But the best way is through experience: learning by living it.

God may place you in deep waters, forcing you to rely totally on Him and thus teaching you firsthand the reality of His faithfulness. This was exactly the method our Lord used with Peter when He came to him walking on the water. Peter stepped out of the boat onto the surface of the water and began to walk toward Jesus. "But seeing the wind, he became afraid, and beginning to sink, he cried out, saying, 'Lord, save me!' And immediately Jesus stretched out His hand and took hold of him, and said to him, 'O you of little faith, why did you doubt?'" (Matthew 14:30-31).

Peter had faith in Jesus, but the Lord knew his heart. He knew that Peter's faith in Him had to be strengthened. The only way He could really teach Peter was to allow him to be in a situation where he would be forced to trust in no one else but the Lord. This is precisely what we need as well.

If we ask God to reveal more about His character to us, then we'd better be ready to learn, no matter what method He uses to teach us. If we are teachers of His Word, He may choose a more difficult path for us to further cleanse and strengthen our lives. After all, if we are to represent the Lord as His ambassadors, our lives need to illustrate His character as closely as possible. For He will hold us accountable for what we say and do: "Let not many of you become teachers, my brethren, knowing that as such we shall incur a stricter judgment" (James 3:1).

Knowing God through a love relationship will definitely cost us one way or the other. But no adversity we encounter, if it is for the glory of God and for our edification, will be significant in any measure when compared with the triumph and glory that is ours throughout eternity. That is why Paul could say without hesitation:

> Whatever things were gain to me, those things I have counted as loss for the sake of Christ. More than that, I count all things to be loss in view of the surpassing value of knowing Christ Jesus my Lord, for whom I have suffered the loss of all things, and count them but rubbish in order that I may gain Christ. (Philippians 3:7-8)

* * *

It has always been an interest of mine to read the biographies of men and women who have endured faithfully for the Lord through the most difficult of circumstances. Reading about their victories and defeats, trials and errors, successes and failures, strengthens my heart, for it allows me the chance to relate to their experiences. But it seems that the common factor in the lives of all those people who accomplished much for God in their generation was their intimate relationship with God. Some of the greatest decisions for God's work resulted when these dedicated saints were alone with the Lord, affirming their love and submission to Him and seeking His grace and direction for their lives and ministries.

There are, of course, many biblical figures God has provided for us as examples (Moses, Elijah, David, Paul, and our greatest example, our Lord Jesus Christ). But also encouraging to me are some contemporary figures who have labored long and hard for Christ in the face of adversity. Their great love for God and timely acts of devotion have served as the impetus to drive them on in enabling them to declare with Paul, "I press on toward the goal for the prize of the upward call of God in Christ Jesus" (Philippians 3:14).

David Brainerd was a man whose intense love and devotion to God made him one of the most inspiring men of God in his day. He was moved at the age of twenty-five to commit his life to bringing the gospel of Jesus Christ to the American Indians of New England. Brainerd's short-lived missionary experience produced over 130 converts to Jesus Christ. After just five years in missions, Brainerd died from tuberculosis on October 9, 1747. His last days were spent at the home of one of the great preachers of his day, Jonathan Edwards. Edwards invited Brainerd to stay in his home because he wanted his family to observe Brainerd's intense prayer life and devotion to God. Also, Brainerd had been hoping to marry Edwards' daughter, Jerusha. But Jerusha contracted the disease from Brainerd and died some four months later.

David Brainerd's life, though disciplined and godly, had its highs and lows. After enrolling at Yale University, he became disturbed at the shallowness of his religious tutors. His feelings led him to comment privately that one of them had no more grace than a chair, and judged him to be a hypocrite.[1] After refusing to publicly apologize, he was expelled.

But it was during his days at Yale that he heard Ebenezer Pemberton share about the need for missionaries among the American Indians. After his expulsion, Brainerd went to discuss with Pemberton the possibility of working with Indians. He was appointed to work with another missionary to learn the language and culture. But it ended in failure because Brainerd's strong desire for independence caused him to step out in his work alone, unprepared and ignorant of the language.

Brainerd's ineffectiveness, along with the hardships of the wilderness, led to discouragement and depression. He left for a new assignment in Pennsylvania, but the results were similar. Nevertheless, his faith and trust in the One he loved kept him looking forward. His times alone with God were his form of strong encouragement.

Finally, in the summer of 1745, he heard about a group of Indians in New Jersey who were eager to hear the gospel. He moved there, and soon watched the fruits of his labor erupt into revival. The Indians were captivated as they listened to Brainerd preach on the love of God out of 1 John 4:10. "It was very affecting to see the poor Indians, who the other day were hallooing and yelling in their idolatrous feasts and drunken frolics, now crying to God with such importunity for an interest in His dear Son!"[2] Soon, a church was established and more revivals followed. But the strenuous work took its toll on Brainerd. After he contracted tuberculosis, he completed his fourth and final preaching tour.

Brainerd's contribution was not so much in his work with the Indians of Crossweeksung but rather in the impression his personal spiritual life made on missionaries for generations to come. William Cary, the man considered today as "the father of modern missions," was greatly influenced by Brainerd. Henry Martyn spent many hours each day in prayer and devotion to God because of Brainerd's example. He once said this of Brainerd:

> I thought of David Brainerd and ardently desired his devotedness to God. I feel my heart knit to this dear man. I long to be like him. Let me forget the world and be swallowed up in a desire to glorify God.[3]

Jonathan Edwards published a book entitled *The Life and Diary of David Brainerd,* which influenced hundreds to become missionaries. Over just a five-year period, Brainerd, because of his intense love and devotion to God resulting from hours and days of time alone with Him, became a mighty weapon for God in his generation and for generations to come.

* * *

Clarence W. Jones was another person of faith who went through many trials to test that faith. Jones had a vision for missionary radio. In a time when many called radio a "tool of the Devil," Jones stepped out in faith to reach the lost in foreign lands through that medium. After overcoming financial problems and the refusal of several South American countries to permit his "Protestant broadcasting," the world's first missionary radio program was broadcast live on Christmas Day in 1931, coming from a 250-watt transmitter located in a sheep shed in Quito, Ecuador. At 3 p.m. that day, Jones declared, "Hoy Cristo Jesus Bendice!"[4] Then he began playing the hymn "Great Is Thy Faithfulness." With this introduction, HCJB (Heralding Christ Jesus' Blessings) was now on the air over the Andes.

Perhaps the most significant event to occur in the life of Clarence Jones and HCJB (also known as World Radio Missionary Fellowship) took place some two years later in a tool shed in May of 1933. After a number of checks bounced and the Chicago Gospel Tabernacle, which was the mission's main supporter, went bankrupt, Jones faced the prospect of going off the air.

But, being faithful to the Lord Jesus Christ as his first love, Jones went alone to his tool shed and prayed, "Dear God, are we finding out now that we've made a terrible mistake? Are we to carry on with HCJB, or pack it in and go home?"[5] He spent that entire day without food or interruptions, waiting on the Lord. Jones vividly recalls, "There wasn't any human hope at that time, but there was something in my heart that looked to the Lord to do something."[6]

The Lord did something by answering Jones and encouraging him by giving him confidence that HCJB would continue on the air. Within a few days, Jones arranged for a loan, and a mortgage on a transmitter. Soon HCJB climbed out of its financial uncertainty and has since grown to its present 24-hour-a-day programing, powered by a six-million-watt hydroelectric plant, broadcasting in fifteen different languages. Recently, its president, a personal friend of our family, Ronald Cline, announced the ambitious goal of cooperating with three other radio missionary organizations to reach the entire population of the world by the year 2000.

And to think that from man's perspective, it was all over back in May of 1933! But because of one man's great love and trust in God, and his willingness to seek the Father's strength and direction by valuing the importance of time alone with Him, the Lord has raised up a tremendous ministry that will one day reach across the entire globe.

* * *

While HCJB was beginning its first broadcasts in 1931, halfway around the world there was a woman who had already served thirty-five years doing missionary work in India. Amy Wilson Carmichael would spend a total of fifty-five years in India, authoring thirty-five books and starting a Christian ministry known as the Dohnavur Fellowship.

Born in 1867 to an affluent family in Northern Ireland, Amy got her start in missions working in the inner city of Belfast after her family moved to that city. Her call to missions was, in her mind, a personal "Go ye" from the Lord. Therefore, she had no choice but to obey.[7] As a young single woman, committing her life to missions work caused her to receive some opposition, but she received permission from the Keswick Convention, which supported her.

After a short, unsuccessful stint in Japan, Amy left on her own and headed toward India. It was there in 1901 that she founded the Dohnavur Fellowship, a unique Christian ministry organized to reach children, especially young girls who were secretly sold as temple prostitutes to be "married to the gods." The children were educated and physically cared for at Dohnavur, and special attention was paid to the development of their "Christian character."[8] Over the years, Miss Carmichael's unique ministry rescued and cared for hundreds of children. She was a remarkable woman, whose radiant, Christlike character made her one of the most beloved missionaries ever to work in India.[9]

Amy Carmichael indeed experienced a deep love relationship with the Lord. It was so deep that she forsook marriage. Amy had such a concern for those who made the choice not to be married that she started the Sisters of the Common Life, a Christian order for single women. It was patterned after a fourteenth-century religious community, the Brothers of the Common Life, founded by a Roman Catholic mystic, Gerhard Groot. Christian mysticism was an integral part of the sisterhood. A spiritual union with Christ compensated for the absence of the physical love of marriage. Amy and her "sisters" testified of a deep and satisfying peace.[10]

Amy's relationship with God was her life. It was her driving motivation to endure behind her ministry. Though she chose to be single to better serve God in an era when singleness had many negative connotations, she was at peace within, faithfully serving the Lord and maintaining a love relationship with Him.

Amy understood the importance of spending time alone with God. It was at such a time that the Lord strengthened and encouraged her during a period when she was experiencing tremendous amounts of fear and loneliness. This was the foremost turning point in her life, as she recalled many years later:

> On this day many years ago I went away alone to a cave in the mountain called Arima. I had feelings of fear about the future. That was why I went there to be alone with God. The devil kept on whispering, "It's all right now, but what about afterwards? You are going to be very lonely." And he painted pictures of loneliness—I can see them still. And I turned to my God in a kind of desperation and said, "Lord, what can I do? How can I go on to the end?" And He said, "None of them that trust in Me shall be desolate." That word has been with me ever since. It has been fulfilled to me.[11]

Amy's love for God and her willingness to draw near to Him made her a great servant of the Lord in her generation.

HOW TO SPEND TIME WITH GOD

Now that we have considered the importance of recognizing our need to spend time with God and looked at a few individuals whose lives were productive for the Lord through their devotion to Him, let's move on and look at some ideas for spending personal time with God. In order to orient our thinking, let's consider the devotional words of a man whose writings have been popular worldwide. William Law was an English theologian and devotional writer, born in 1705. He wrote several books and essays in response to the religious "liberalism" of his day.

Law's most valued contribution was a book entitled *A Serious Call to a Devout and Holy Life* (1729). This devotional book became an inspiration to many godly preachers, such as Samuel Johnson, George Whitefield, and Henry Venn. It has become one of my personal favorites. Law presents the argument that if we are serious about following God, we will live as Christians in every activity of life. He maintained that the Christian life was a constant practice of self-denial and humility, forsaking the things of the world, which are in contradiction to the things of God. A Christian's life must be fully lived to the glory of God. Each of us should recognize Him as the sovereign Victor in our life:

> You can make no stand against the assaults of pride, the meek affections of humility can have no place in your soul, till you stop the power of the world over you, and resolve against a blind obedience to its laws.
> The Christian's great conquest over the world is all contained in the mystery of Christ upon the Cross. It was there, and from thence, that He taught all Christians how they were to come out of and conquer the world, and what they were to do in order to be His disciples.[12]

Regarding our time alone with God, sense the mood in prayer that William Law asserts:

> The first thing that you are to do, when you are upon
> your knees, is to shut your eyes, and with a short
> silence let your soul place itself in the presence of
> God; that is, you are to use this, or some other better
> method, to separate yourself from all common
> thoughts, and make your heart as sensible as you can
> of the Divine presence.[13]

Law was certainly a man who knew how to draw near to
God. He knew the importance of trusting in the power of
God for victory over sin, and he understood the need for
being separated from the distractions of the world before
coming to a holy God. Keep Law's counsel in mind as you
consider each of the ideas for spending time with the Lord.

As we pointed out in Chapter 4, spending time alone
with God is a key principle in devoting ourselves to Him
through our worship, prayer, and personal study. The following list of devotional ideas are primarily designed as
activities you can do by yourself—just between you and the
Lord. You may consider doing some of them with a partner
or even a third person. If another person or two will serve as
an aid to your worship, by all means include them. But if
there is the potential for distraction, go it alone.

It is important to remember that these activities are
specifically designed for personal devotional and prayer
times, not so much for personal Bible study. They are
intended to help us express our love to God. (For personal
Bible study ideas, consult your nearest Christian bookstore.
There are vast resources of material available.)

Activities
    Alphabet praise
    Building an altar to God
    Day of prayer, worship, and meditation

Love poems and love letters
Songs of praise and songs of worship
Meditation
Audio-visual praise presentation
Prayer-worship diary-log
Fasting
Sunrise rendezvous
Mountain and country hikes
Overnight and weekend retreats

Alphabet praise is an encouraging activity that you can do over and over again. Sit down with paper and pencil and write down words beginning with all the letters of the alphabet describing your love, honor, and respect for God (for example, awesome, blessed, comfort . . . zeal). It is especially exciting to do this entire exercise one day, then do it again a month later and compare your words. It could give you some insight into your spiritual growth. In any event, it can be a very meaningful experience that will cause you to think deeply about the Lord.

Building an altar to God is a powerful activity. Its purpose is twofold: (1) to cause us to reflect on the sacrifice of Jesus Christ for the forgiveness of our sins (a memorial—Joshua 22:26-27, Hebrews 13:10) and (2) to serve as a reminder to us to commit our total person to God for His glory and enjoyment (worship and praise—Genesis 13:4,18; 22:9; 26:25).

Although altars played a role in many heathen religions and although they were not recognized by the New Testament Church, there is much evidence to indicate that God established the idea of the altar with man very early as a means of approaching Him. The altar played a significant role throughout the Old Testament as a symbol of worship and praise to the true God. For us today, building an altar in the quiet presence of our God can certainly serve as a powerful expression of our worship and adoration of Him.

In terms of construction, the shapes, sizes, and materials varied in Old Testament times (although sometimes God stated how an altar was to be made, including the materials to be used). Some were made with dirt, some with stone. Some were just a pile of rocks (1 Kings 18:31), and one consisted of just one rock (1 Samuel 14:33-35). An altar to God today could be designed with just about any kind of construction, as long as it serves as a reminder for us to reflect on the sacrifice of Jesus Christ for our sins and an aid to our praise and worship. I have piled rocks beside a stream or on mountain ledges, calling them my altar of praise, symbolizing my commitment to God. Building an altar can be something you experience alone or something you enjoy with other people. It is an expression of love and devotion that every Christian should try at least once.

A day of prayer, worship, and meditation is simply an six-to-twelve-hour period you spend alone with God. It involves prayer, devotion (using many of the activities listed in this chapter), and personal Bible study. It is an activity I personally try to do at least four or five times a year.

Its value is that it breaks us away from the pressures of daily living and refreshes our spiritual condition by renewing our heart and our attitude. For myself, the pressures of the ministry can sometimes cause me to drift in my walk with God because of administrative duties and the needs of other people. My personal daily time with God certainly keeps me going, but every now and then, a full day alone with God allows me the freedom to spend a greater amount of time getting to know Him better, without looking at my watch or worrying about schedules.

Love poems and love letters are fun and exciting to do. They are a form of our love and devotion expressed to God in a very intimate way.

With paper and pencil, write down your feelings for God. Share with Him your love, dreams, and desires, and how they have been impacted by His love. You may not finish a poem or letter in just one day (since you may have only five or ten minutes a day for devotion to God), so spread it out over a week or two, accomplishing a little each day. When you finish a letter, share it with other people, for it may encourage others.

I shared this idea with the high school group I was leading while finishing up my work at seminary. One young girl became inspired with the idea, and over the years since then, she has written hundreds of poems to the Lord. She has sent me several and has put them in a devotional book for other people to see. It is an activity that has nurtured her love for God in a very profound way.

Songs of praise and songs of worship are very similar to love poems and love letters except that music is added and the words are sung. One does not need to prove the value of such devotional worship. Just reading portions of the book of Psalms will reveal its importance in the lives of people as they worshiped and praised God.

But one thing about songs of worship and praise, unlike love poems and letters, is that we can also take Scripture and apply music to it and express it to God. Or we can sing Scripture verses without musical accompaniment. Either way, songs of praise and worship can be a meaningful form of expressing our hearts to God.

In my college days, I played in a Christian musical group with a good friend of mine, Kevin Downing. Together we put music to Psalm 46. It became our most worshipful and influential song. Our collaboration was simply the result of wanting to express our love to God in song.

Meditation is a quiet exercise in which we remove all

distractions and dwell on the greatness and holiness of God, together with His presence in our lives. It may be a period of two or three minutes, or as long as two or three hours. The longer the period of time, the more difficult it is to concentrate. Therefore, it is important that we choose a period of time that will benefit us the most and keep us from mental drifting. I would suggest reading a few psalms to begin your meditation. I usually include a short period of meditation in every devotional period.

An audio-visual praise presentation involves both our time and our money. But it can serve as one of the more rewarding activities of our devotional life. It is an activity that involves our creativity, and may also involve the gifts and talents of several other people.

Simply stated, an audio-visual praise (and worship) presentation is putting the photography of images, landscapes, and people to music. It is designed to enhance our praise and worship of God by capturing inspirational visual displays of God's creation enhanced by inspirational music.

There are several Christian organizations currently using such presentations in promoting their work. But it can also be a very spiritually rewarding experience as a personal devotional activity. The actual planning and completion of the presentation alone will do much toward causing us to more closely reflect on the Lord. I have had the opportunity to create three such presentations over the years. Not only did they enhance my devotional and spiritual life but also they served as encouragements to friends I was able to share them with.

It may take a month or two to complete such a project. But as with writing poetry or songs to the Lord, do a little each devotional period. Or perhaps you could incorporate it within a day of prayer or weekend pilgrimage. It is a very creative worship experience.

A *prayer-worship diary-log* should be a part of every devotional and prayer period. It is a notebook in which we record our praises, prayer requests and answers, and noteworthy spiritual occurrences. The value in such a log is seeing how God has worked in the past (answered prayer) and in the present (praises). Here is an example of what a log may look like:

Praise, prayers, answers, occurrences	Date of prayer request	Date answered	Comments; results
John has been accepted. He got the job he wanted.		10/14	John is praising God.
Bill's brother to receive Christ	10/14		
For Sue's tumor to be benign	10/16	10/18	It was benign.
I learned the difference between remorse and repentance		10/17	It has helped my understanding.
Kathy praying for acceptance into university	10/17	12/14	God said no.

Fasting is abstinence from food and drink over a period of time. It could be as brief as eight hours, or as long as a few days, though our Lord miraculously survived forty days in the wilderness.

In the Old Testament, there are many examples of

fasting as primarily a sign of mourning over sin. In the New Testament, there are several references to fasting. In Luke 2:37, there is a reference to Anna: "A widow . . . the age of eighty-four . . . never left the temple, serving night and day with fastings and prayers."

Because our Lord never said anything to commend fasting and the Church never really promoted it (although it practiced it), some people feel that fasting is merely a carry-over from Judaism. But for us, its value is in the aspect of sacrifice. Our need for food makes us constantly aware of the Lord. We place ourselves in reverence to God when we abstain from the pleasures of food and drink. There is no asceticism intended, but rather it is the personal, quiet expression of selflessness to God.

A sunrise rendezvous as well as *mountain and country hikes* can be some of the more exhilarating devotional activities we can do. They allow us to "feel" the Lord's presence through His creation without distractions. It is a very moving experience to get up before sunrise and hike to a secluded area and talk with the Lord as the sun rises over the horizon. It can be just as inspiring to walk through a forest, along a stream, or up a mountain concentrating on the greatness of God. These activities have certainly provided some of the more rewarding devotional times in my life, especially since I can include other devotional activities such as building an altar or writing a poem or song.

Overnight and weekend retreats are devotional activities that allow us a greater length of time to spend with God. They can be shared with your husband or wife, your youth group or Bible study group.

I usually design my retreats to accomplish a few specific devotional activities alone with a designated Bible study, centered around a specific theme, such as worship, loyalty, or submission. Whatever you do, whether it is a retreat for you alone or a retreat with several other people, make it a time of spiritual retrospect and evaluation coupled with devotional activities designed to encourage a closer walk with God.

Hopefully, some of these suggestions may be helpful to your prayer and devotional life. Of course, devotional activities are not limited to these ideas, just to your creative imagination. Devotion is our expression of our total self in love with God. Read the words of William Law:

> Devotion is neither private nor public prayer; but prayers, whether private or public, are particular parts or instances of devotion. Devotion signifies a life given, or devoted, to God.
>
> He, therefore, is the devout man, who lives no longer to his own will, or the way and spirit of the world, but to the whole will of God; who considers God in everything, who serves God in everything, who makes all the parts of his common life parts of piety, by doing everything in the Name of God, and under such rules as are conformable to His glory.
>
> We readily acknowledge that God alone is to be the rule and measure of our prayers; that in them we are to look wholly unto Him, and act wholly for Him.[14]

As we develop our love relationship with the Lord, let us not forget our time alone with Him. Let us not forget that we need Him more than anything in this world.

NOTES:
   1. Ruth A. Tucker, *From Jerusalem to Irian Jaya* (Grand Rapids: Zondervan, 1983), page 90.
   2. Tucker, *From Jerusalem to Irian Jaya*, page 93.
   3. Tucker, *From Jerusalem to Irian Jaya*, page 133.
   4. Lois Neely, *Come Up to This Mountain* (Wheaton: Tyndale, 1982), page 88.
   5. Neely, *Come Up to This Mountain*, page 108.
   6. Neely, *Come Up to This Mountain*, page 108.

7. Tucker, *From Jerusalem to Irian Jaya*, page 239.
8. Tucker, *From Jerusalem to Irian Jaya*, page 241.
9. Tucker, *From Jerusalem to Irian Jaya*, page 239.
10. Tucker, *From Jerusalem to Irian Jaya*, page 242.
11. Frank Houghton, *Amy Carmichael of Dohnavur* (London: Society for the Propagation of Christian Knowledge, 1954), page 62.
12. William Law, *A Serious Call to a Devout and Holy Life* (Wilton: Morehouse-Barlow, 1982), pages 41-42.
13. Law, *A Serious Call*, pages 34-35.
14. Law, *A Serious Call*, page 7.

CHAPTER SIX

Fellowship

*In the triangle of love between
ourselves, God, and other people,
is found the secret of existence, and
the best foretaste, I suspect, that we
can have on earth of what heaven
will probably be like.*
SAMUEL M. SHOEMAKER

After accepting the call to my first ministry position right out
of seminary, Janet and I moved to Arizona and purchased a
home not far from the church. The house was situated on a
half-acre lot lined with pine trees and large boulders, something Prescott had in abundance. The only thing the house
lacked was a garage and a driveway. Coming from southern
California, we didn't consider a house quite complete without a garage and a concrete driveway. But we liked the
house, and we made plans to build on a garage and a
driveway. I had a background in carpentry, and also some
good friends who moved with us to Prescott were willing to
lend a hand.

So, Mark and I began our work—hoisting the walls and raising the roof. Soon the only thing left was the concrete floor and driveway. Not being confident of my concrete finishing ability, I hired the services of a man who had a good reputation both as a finisher and as a Christian.

Over lunch on his first day on the job, Frank and I struck up a conversation about "religion." He seemed interested in my spiritual background and my seminary experience. We also shared individual experiences about God's grace and goodness, as well as what He was currently doing in our lives.

As Frank shared, I noticed that he never referred to any church, pastor, Bible teacher, or book (even the Bible) that had encouraged his spiritual life. It was always what *he* believed. Finally, I asked him what church he attended. His response was immediate and to the point: "I don't attend any church!" At his response, I thought for a moment that I had offended him. "But why would it offend him?" I thought to myself. After all, I was not attempting to be nosey or personal, nor was I about to plug my own church.

Well, I did not have to speculate much longer, for he spoke up and began to defend his statement to me. He shared a number of reasons why involvement in a church and its people is not necessary for salvation or spirituality. He also said that there were too many hypocrites in churches and that his style of individual worship was far more pleasing to God.

You can probably guess that my next question to him was, "How would you describe your style of worship?" He thought for a moment, then rubbed his cheek and said, "It's a personal thing between me and God. I don't need a church or other people to tell me how to be a good Christian."

I have never forgotten that statement because it has

always bothered me. How could anyone claim in one breath that he loved the Lord and was growing in Him but that all churches were filled with hypocrites and that he didn't need the fellowship of Christians?

I decided to quickly conclude the conversation with Frank because I felt myself wanting to roll up my sleeves and talk with him. I also sensed that he was ready for an argument because he maintained a defensive tone in his voice.

Two days later, Frank was completing his work on my driveway. I decided that at the appropriate time, I would chat with him about his earlier statement regarding his "worship" practices. Later that afternoon, we talked. I shared with Frank that I was puzzled about how he could justify his individual worship since, from my understanding, Scripture seemed to indicate that both were important: individual and corporate worship, as well as the corporate fellowship of believers. I stated that due to the numerous references to the Body of Christ in Scripture, it seemed that God did not desire believers to live a solo faith.

He then stopped me and told me that this was where he and I "parted waters." He said that he interpreted the Bible his way and that I should not try to impress my biblical interpretation on other people.

I agreed not to pursue it any longer, but felt frustrated. I had approached him as tactfully as I could. My only desire was to encourage him to explore what the Bible teaches about fellowship and its importance in relation to our love for God and our spiritual growth.

* * *

What is fellowship? Is it for everyone, including unbelievers? Must it be a necessary part of our Christian life? How will fellowship help develop our love relationship with God?

Furthermore, can a believer like Frank mature in the Christian life without it? Well, there are certainly a great variety of books and materials on the market today that will assist a Christian in his understanding of fellowship and how it applies to his life. Yet it has become a word used quite loosely in many Christian circles.

To one person, fellowship is simply a social gathering of believers over coffee and donuts. To another, fellowship is strictly spiritual interaction between believers who have a common doctrinal background. And to still another, fellowship is what we have in common with the Lord and other believers as a result of our confession of faith in Him.

Without sounding too compromising, true biblical fellowship could be the combination of all three of these definitions. Fellowship is the usual translation of the Greek word *koinōnia.* Fellowship is "a partnership; possessing things in common; a belonging in common to."[1] It is a sharing of common interests or common goals.

As believers, we have the promise of eternal life. Therefore, we share in eternal life that comes from the Father. We have a oneness in faith with each other. John gives us a description of this fellowship:

> What we have seen and heard we proclaim to you
> also, that you also may have fellowship with us; and
> indeed our fellowship is with the Father, and with His
> Son Jesus Christ. (1 John 1:3)

According to John, fellowship (*koinōnia*) is the common bond we have with each other, conditional on our first experiencing a bond of fellowship with the Father through Jesus Christ.

How does a believer experience this fellowship with the Father that will lead to fellowship with believers? One passage that will help our understanding is 2 Corinthians 13:14, an interesting Pauline benediction: "The grace of the Lord Jesus Christ, and the love of God, and the fellowship of the Holy Spirit, be with you all." The phrase "fellowship of the Holy Spirit" does not imply companionship with the Holy Spirit. Rather, as we draw near to God with our heart and mind fixed totally on Him, the Holy Spirit, by His work, makes our fellowship possible with the Lord and with other believers. It is the Spirit's task to deal with our thoughts and attitudes individually in order to prepare us to commune with the Father and also with other believers in a godly manner. Thus, "fellowship of the Holy Spirit" means our cooperation with the Spirit of God as we prepare our hearts to draw near to God and to exhibit love and fellowship toward other believers.

John provides for us the true tests of fellowship by listing three false assumptions claimed by those who boast of their knowledge and fellowship with God:

> If we say that we have fellowship with Him and yet
>   walk in the darkness, we lie and do not practice
>   the truth. . . .
> If we say that we have no sin, we are deceiving
>   ourselves, and the truth is not in us. . . .
> If we say that we have not sinned, we make Him a liar,
>   and His word is not in us. (1 John 1:6,8,10)

Therefore, in order to have fellowship with God and with other believers, we must walk in the light, not in darkness, since God is light. Whereas light is a symbol (used by John several times: John 1:4, 8:12, 9:5) of God's purity and holiness, we walk in the light when we live in obedience to Him. While speaking about a relationship between believers and unbelievers, Paul asks rhetorically, "What fellowship has light with darkness?" (2 Corinthians 6:14).

(b) We must have fellowship with other believers because we have been cleansed of our sins by the subsequent shedding of the blood of Jesus Christ. We share this common bond of deliverance from sin:

> If we walk in the light as He Himself is in the light, we have fellowship with one another, and the blood of Jesus His Son cleanses us from all sin. (1 John 1:7)

(c) Because Jesus made confession of sin necessary for forgiveness, through our fellowship we must confess our sins to God and to other believers (James 5:16). (Confessing our sins to someone else is not necessarily a condition for forgiveness, unless we have sinned against another brother.) We have been given the promise that God is faithful and righteous to forgive our sins through Christ, who is our advocate and the sacrifice for our sins.

> If we confess our sins, He is faithful and righteous to forgive us our sins and to cleanse us from all unrighteousness. . . . He Himself is the propitiation for our sins; and not for ours only, but also for those of the whole world. (1 John 1:9, 2:2)

With these points in mind, we can safely summarize fellowship with the three following conclusions:

(1) True fellowship is only for the believer who is actively walking in love and obedience (in the light) to God.

(2) Our fellowship with God and the brethren is maintained by our repentance and confession of sin through the continual cleansing of the blood of Jesus, for the sting of sin destroys fellowship.

(3) Our fellowship with the Lord is displayed through

our love for the brethren.

With these conclusions about fellowship in mind, one can easily understand why John later relates our love for the brethren with our love for God: "By this we know that we love the children of God, when we love God and observe His commandments" (1 John 5:2). Our love for the brethren is a byproduct of our true love for God. Therefore, the deeper and more enduring our love for God, the stronger our fellowship with Him and the brethren. And conversely, as our love and fellowship with the brethren grows stronger, so does our love for God (1 John 4:7-10). Hence, our fellowship with the brethren becomes a confirmation of our fellowship and love for God.

Before we explore in more depth how our fellowship with other believers will help develop a more dynamic love for God, let us first consider some distinctive functions of New Testament fellowship. These distinctives will help clarify the differences in fellowship that we may observe in our churches. They will also provide a profile of biblical fellowship that we can subscribe to, both social and spiritual.

NEW TESTAMENT FELLOWSHIP

In Hebrews 10:22-25, the author states three exhortations that should stir certain actions within the fellowship of believers as a result of Christ's sacrifice: (1) "Let us draw near with a sincere heart"; (2) "Let us hold fast the confession of our hope"; and (3) "Let us consider how to stimulate one another to love and good deeds."

Along with these three exhortations comes the command that we are not to forsake "our assembling together" (Hebrews 10:25). We can conclude that in our assembling together, our fellowship should provoke us to draw near to God with sincere hearts, to hold fast to our hope in Him, and to stimulate one another to love and good deeds.

There are two points in this passage that need to be stressed. First, the expression "one another" is significant because although it is a short phrase used widely throughout the New Testament, it is found only once in the book of Hebrews. In 10:24, "one another" refers to activity initiated by believers, not necessarily by the appointed direction of a leader. In other words, *all* believers are to take the initiative to encourage and stimulate one another to action.

Many of us attend church expecting the leadership to ignite our fellowship with other believers and to prompt our worship with the Lord. From this perspective, we can develop an "entertain me" attitude. But in light of Hebrews 10:22-25, this is certainly an unbiblical attitude. We must recognize that God expects all of us to be responsible to initiate a certain kind of fellowship: a fellowship that causes us to draw near to God with sincere hearts, to provoke us to hold fast to our hope in Him, and to stimulate each other to love and good deeds.

Second, notice that we have been called to *provoke* one another to *love*. This is one of the more important obligations we have in our relationships with one another (Romans 12:10; Hebrews 10:24, 13:1; 1 Peter 1:22). Because of this obligation, our fellowship with one another becomes a vital part of our daily Christian life (Hebrews 3:13). We continually need the input and encouragement, as well as the admonition and correction, from like-minded believers who are themselves in fellowship with the Lord and the brethren. Such relationships could only be maintained in an attitude of love.

Because God chooses to work through His people, to deny having fellowship with other believers is to deny the Lord a means of His direction, correction, encouragement, and love.

In terms of function, New Testament fellowship can be

distinguished by two types: (1) Interpersonal or social fellowship and (2) Dynamic spiritual fellowship.

* * *

Interpersonal or social fellowship is not necessarily referring to the "coffee and donuts" socializing we see in our churches, although that can be a part of it. That type of coffee fellowship rarely ventures beyond surface talk.

Rather, what we are talking about here is the warm and trusting interpersonal friendships we develop with other believers out of our mutual love of Christ and our earnest desire to grow in Him (2 Corinthians 6:5; Hebrews 3:13; 1 John 4:21, 5:2). These are the edifying friendships based on *agapē* love, friendships that may evolve from outside the walls of the church but are nevertheless inside the Body of Christ. They can occur over meals or in prayer groups. They can take place in Sunday school gatherings or in a night of dinner and sharing between Christians.

In His journeys, Jesus would often stop in and fellowship with Martha, Mary, and Lazarus over meals (Luke 10:38-42, John 12:1-3). Their times together were examples of genuine care and support for one another. Jesus dearly loved them and felt close to them (John 11:5).

Paul's relationship with Epaphras, the pastor of the church at Colossae, was likewise a very close fellowship. He brought support and encouragement to Paul during his first imprisonment in Rome. He was Paul's "fellow bond-servant" (Colossians 1:7). Epaphras was Paul's fellow prisoner and a faithful minister. Paul also experienced a deep fellowship with Apollos, who was one of his trusted friends and companions. Apollos was an eloquent and educated speaker whose fervency for the Lord was an encouragement to Paul throughout Paul's ministry (Acts 18:24-25, 1 Corinthians 16:2, Titus 3:13).

Janet and I have several close friends we fellowship with socially. Our relationships together bring enthusiasm and encouragement to our lives. Whether we go out to dinner or stay home and eat popcorn over *Bible Trivia,* the fellowship we enjoy together is spiritually stimulating and marked by our common bond in Jesus Christ.

Bonding between believers in interpersonal fellowship seems to take place more readily than bonding in relationships outside of Christ. It is almost like a built-in confidence we have in each other that allows us to experience closeness in a shorter length of time. Because of Christ living in us, there is an established element of trust binding our hearts. This allows us more freedom to readily express our lives to one another without fear of judgment or rejection.

This instant bond was one of the primary reasons for a close fellowship I developed with a pastor friend in Oregon several years ago. Dave Boldt pastored a church about an hour's drive from my home. We developed a friendship through the meetings held monthly by our ministerial association. I soon learned that Dave was one of those special individuals who could minister to the needs of people with great discernment. He had a deep conviction for nurturing and restoring the brethren.

After I resigned my position at a church in the general area, Dave made himself available to my wife and me for prayer, counsel, and fellowship. He seemed to understand the sense of loss and loneliness Janet and I were feeling after being separated from those we had grown to love and care for in our ministry.

Dave's fellowship with us brought encouragement to our lives and hope to our future. It was a powerful example to us of loving the brethren in deed and truth. He reached out to us in love, resulting in true fellowship impelled by our common bond as believers in Jesus Christ.

I believe that true interpersonal fellowship never fades when Christian brothers and sisters are separated by time. It merely picks up where it left off. Since it is the love of God that binds believers together, and the love of God is the same yesterday, today, and forever, His love in us (which we have invested in others through fellowship) will remain strong—even when we are separated over space and time. My friend Dave and I are separated by over a thousand miles, but when we greet each other, it's as if we have been together every day the previous year.

Interpersonal fellowship is certainly one of the special byproducts of our love for God. But our fellowship with others must never be viewed as an "extra" that we can choose to take or leave. Rather, it is an essential element to our growth and maturity in Christ.

* * *

Dynamic spiritual fellowship refers to the mutual spiritual edification of believers, assembled together for the purposes of instruction, correction, praise, and worship (Acts 2:42-47, 5:12). It is the gathering together of the Body of Christ, a recognition that all believers are of the same household of faith.

Paul talked about the "barrier of the dividing wall" that existed as a negative relationship between the Jew and the Gentile (Ephesians 2:14). There was an actual wall dividing the Court of the Jews from the Court of the Gentiles in the Temple. But because of Jesus Christ, the wall has been knocked down (figuratively), allowing both Christian Jew and Christian Gentile to be united in the Body of Christ, in fellowship with one another.

> So then you are no longer strangers and aliens, but you are fellow-citizens with the saints, and are of

> God's household. . . . In [Jesus Christ] you also are
> being built together into a dwelling of God in the
> Spirit. (Ephesians 2:19,22)

This is the dynamic of spiritual fellowship that unites young
and old, rich and poor, black and white. This kind of
powerful fellowship molds into one Body people who may
have nothing in common from the world's perspective, but
everything in common through Jesus Christ. It is a fellowship that knows no barriers.

Perhaps one of the more profound yet unheralded
New Testament examples of dynamic spiritual fellowship
was the relationship between two of the apostles: Matthew
the tax-gatherer and Simon the Zealot.

Matthew was heavily involved in his trade of collecting
taxes for the government of Rome when Jesus approached
him and said, "Follow Me!" (Matthew 9:9). Matthew's trade
was, to say the least, detestable in the eyes of most Jews. Not
only did a tax-gatherer collect dues and fees from his own
people (making him appear to be traitor to his people), but
also the majority of tax-gatherers were thieves and crooks
because they added a percentage to the charges for themselves. What was the attitude of the Jews toward a tax-
gatherer?

> The public ostracized him. His neighbors shunned
> him. The church people had made it clear how they
> felt. They looked down on him as they did a prosti-
> tute. That was utterly unfair. "Collaborator with
> Rome," they charged; "traitor to Israel."[3]

It was quite a bold step for our Lord to call a man whose
trade held such a reputation. But thankfully, the Lord
knows the hearts of men. He knew Matthew's potential.

Jesus knew what Matthew was going to become for Him. And anyway, it was not Jesus' objective to call out the "pure and the self-righteous." As He declared to the Pharisees who were annoyed by His dining with tax-gatherers and sinners, "I did not come to call the righteous, but sinners" (Matthew 9:13). Matthew was just the right man to become one of the twelve men who would later turn their world upside-down (Acts 17:6).

Simon of Canaan, better known as Simon the Zealot, was the eleventh apostle listed in the Twelve. Not much is known about him except what we can derive from his nickname. He was called "the Zealot" because of his membership in a fanatical political group known as the Zealots. They were a group of Jews dedicated to the overthrow of the Roman government from Palestine. Because national freedom for Israel was their primary objective, if it was aided by violent means, then so much the better. Simon, as a member of such a group, was a rebel full of zeal for his country and his cause.

Now let us compare these two apostles: Matthew the tax-gatherer and Simon the Zealot:

> Compare Simon and Matthew. Simon, the Zealot, who wanted to overthrow the Roman Government and Matthew the tax-gatherer, who worked hand-in-glove with Rome. Simon, the tax hater and Matthew the tax collector. Simon, the Jewish patriot, and Matthew who seemed to everyone unpatriotic. Can you imagine these two hotheads in the same group?[4]

Because of the power and love of Jesus Christ, Matthew and Simon, through the dynamic spiritual fellowship they experienced in Christ, could bury their respective causes and differences, and walk together in one accord under the banner of God's love. Though together they probably did not experience close interpersonal fellowship, as believers in Jesus Christ, they certainly enjoyed spiritual fellowship that was edifying both for them and for the Body of Christ (Acts 1:13-14, 2:42, 6:4).

Back when I was a student at Talbot Theological Seminary, one day in chapel I heard an interesting story about fellowship. Dr. Louis Talbot was attending a fellowship dinner while conducting some meetings in Chicago. At this dinner were Christian representatives from several nations. Presiding over the dinner was a Christian Jew. Next to him sat a German. A Japanese sat next to a Chinese. Talbot, an Englishman, sat next to an Irishman. An Austrian sat next to an Italian. They were all seated around a large table. Over dinner, there was not a word of political slur or prejudice, for they were experiencing deep spiritual fellowship united by one Spirit in Christ. At the end of the dinner, they all stood, joined hands, and sang "Blest Be the Tie That Binds."

Such fellowship could never happen in the lives of people whose love and fellowship with the Lord was shallow, for their love for the brethren would likewise be shallow. Dr. Talbot and his friends loudly declared by their actions toward one another John's command to us: "Beloved, let us love one another, for love is from God; and every one who loves is born of God and knows God" (1 John 4:7).

THE RESULT OF FELLOWSHIP

I think one of the major factors that influenced me toward the Lord as a nonbeliever was the sincere expression of love I observed between Christians. I was continually impressed by the genuine care and concern they exhibited toward each other, even when they were not well acquainted with each other. Their fellowship resembled a warm, intimate family relationship. And this fellowship poured itself out in love to all people, not just to other believers.

I discovered this love in a very real way from an acquaintance of mine. Halfway through my first year in college, I bumped into an old high school classmate of mine. Mark and I had never been good friends. In fact, because we had competed against each other for similar positions on the football and basketball teams throughout our high school years, we did not have the fondest memories of each other. But when I saw Mark, I immediately observed that there was something different about him. When we first noticed each other, he approached me and greeted me with a big smile and a firm handshake. He had never done that before! To say the least, I was dumbfounded.

As we stood together and talked, Mark did not sound as I had remembered him, somewhat cocky and proud. In fact, he seemed to be truly concerned with me and what I was doing. I began to wonder if I was really talking to the Mark I knew in high school or someone else.

Through the course of our conversation, I learned what had caused his change. The previous summer, he attended a youth camp and became a Christian. He was now regularly attending a church and was involved in a home Bible study with some other friends. From what I observed, his character was totally different. And for such a noticeable change, I was forced to conclude that his Christianity was no myth.

Mark's example was just one of the many examples God brought into my life prior to my conversion, but it was indeed Mark's example that raised my curiosity enough to motivate me to attend a Bible study near my home. In that Bible study I felt the reality of the love of Christ permeating through Christians who were thoroughly enjoying their fellowship with each other. The example of their love and care for each other and their love for God finally caused me to doubt no longer. Just a few weeks after entering Bible study, I received Christ on August 23, 1972.

My story is not so unusual. I have heard many testimonies of people drawn to the Lord because of the examples of love and fellowship they witnessed in Christian relationships. While it is true that some social forms of "fellowship" may even do harm to the cause of the gospel (e.g., certain cluster groups, cliques, etc.), the genuine New Testament form of fellowship is a powerful force in causing people to fall in love with God.

The fellowship of believers is a graphic testimony of the love and grace of God, pouring itself into the life of every believer. It is the vivid display of the indwelling presence of Christ, who transforms every believer into a new creation (2 Corinthians 5:17). Fellowship is the avenue of our expression of love, joy, peace, and contentment declaring the reality of God to an unbelieving world. It is the wonderful condition in which we can live peacefully and joyously with other believers.

Throughout the New Testament, evidences of fellowship among believers can be seen in instances of mutual comfort and encouragement. Their fellowship served to strengthen their love for God, which made it easier for them to endure through the difficult trials of their time.

Returning from their first missionary journey, Paul and Barnabas came back through the cities of Lystra, Iconium, and Antioch "strengthening the souls of the disciples, encouraging them to continue in the faith, and saying, 'Through many tribulations we must enter the kingdom of God'" (Acts 14:22). On Paul's second missionary journey, he and Silas continued the same approach in Syria and Cilicia (Acts 15:41), and in Derbe, and again in Lystra, and Iconium (Acts 16:1-5).

No doubt the Philippian jailer was influenced to receive Christ by the strong fellowship he witnessed in Paul and Silas as they prayed and sang together while in a prison cell (Acts 16:24-34). And Crispus, the leader of a synagogue next door to the home of a devout Christian, Titius Justus, most likely witnessed and heard the strong faith and fellowship of Titius' household.

At the conclusion of his second missionary journey, Paul went before the church at Jerusalem and related "one by one the things which God had done among the Gentiles through his ministry. And when they heard it they began glorifying God" (Acts 21:19-20).

Scripture is filled with instances of fellowship and the results of it, not only in the lives of believers but also in its impact in the world. There can be no doubt that true biblical fellowship—drawing His people to one another— is one of God's primary means of drawing all people to Himself. In the fellowship of Christians, God's love, grace, faithfulness, and reality become clearly evident, not by human emotion or intuition generated by human intellect but solely by the Holy Spirit of God.

NOTES:
1. Wuest, *Word Studies,* Volume 3, page 33.
2. Wuest, *Word Studies,* (Volume 3, page 98.
3. H.S. Vigeveno, *13 Men Who Changed the World* (Ventura: Regal Books, 1986), page 47.
4. Vigeveno, *13 Men,* page 60.

PART II

*Evidences of a
Love Relationship*

CHAPTER SEVEN

Joy and Peace

The word "joy" is too great and grand to be confused with the superficial thing we call happiness. It was joy and peace which Jesus said He left men in His will.
KIRBY PAGE

Joy and peace. Hmm? Sounds like the latest happily-ever-after Hollywood script. Or the rewards for the satisfactory completion of one of the dozen self-help seminars offered at the local auditorium—that is, after you have paid the $350 for the thirty-day kit that has everything to guarantee you a perfect, tranquil life.

Whatever their use, these two elusive virtues—joy and peace—are sought by people the world over. Many will do almost anything to experience them in their lives. Some may explore the use of drugs and alcohol. Others will dabble in illicit social or sexual behavior. Still others will become obsessed with the need for money to purchase their "happiness."

Our culture is swamped with advertising slogans and slick publicity campaigns promoting products designed to provide us with temporary moments of enjoyment and pleasure—even if these products are harmful to our bodies or unproven in the laboratory. In a society that is moving increasingly farther from its dependence on God, people are talking louder and louder about the desperate need for peace and happiness. Perhaps that unforgettable song popularized by Judy Garland in the motion picture *The Wizard of Oz* reflects our futile attempts of trying to achieve joy and peace on our own. "Somewhere Over the Rainbow" expresses the desire to escape to some faraway place where problems "melt like lemon drops," a utopia of peace and happiness where bluebirds fly over the rainbow, and we find ourselves asking, "Why, oh why, can't I?"

Did Miss Garland ever find her perfect world? Did she ever achieve an inward peace to help her endure through the struggles of life? Apparently not. She later took her own life—a life that to many appeared happy and fulfilled. Unfortunately, what she appeared to have was not what she needed. She became disenchanted and disillusioned with life.

As Christians, what should we expect from joy and peace? Should we live our lives in an eternal state of bliss, smiling from ear to ear in the face of every trial? Are we supposed to forever exhibit complete peace, regardless of the severity of the situation, in order to prove to ourselves and others that we are mentally fit and strong in the Lord? How does a love relationship with God affect the way we express joy and peace in our lives?

Many times I hear Christians talk about their love for God, and the joy and peace they have through Him. Yet I have to scratch my head in wonder after hearing these same people continually lament their feelings of anxiety and fear every other week in prayer group. Have they forgotten that the joy of the Lord is their strength (Nehemiah 8:10), and that their privilege as believers allows them to claim and rest in "the peace of God, which surpasses all comprehension, [which guards their] hearts and . . . minds in Christ Jesus"? (Philippians 4:7). Perhaps they have confused God's joy and peace with the world's view of joy and peace.

As Christians, it is very important that we do not evaluate or measure God's responses to our prayers with secular definitions. Judging the acts of God with definitions manufactured to judge the things of the world limits both God and our understanding of why He does what He does. It also causes us to lose sight of God's viewpoint, thus allowing us to potentially lose perspective in our position in Christ.

For example, say that we, as Christians, ask the Lord for peace in our lives while we are enduring through turbulent situations. If we have in mind the world's view of peace, we might expect God to answer our prayer by putting a quick halt to our problems and leading us down the gentle, tranquil path of no resistance and no more trials. But God in His perfect wisdom may choose to allow us to continue in a difficult situation a little bit longer in order to glorify Him. And He does answer our prayer (His way) by providing us a special measure of His peace, which is intended to guard our hearts and minds against anxiety and fear (Philippians 4:7). Thus, we are better able to endure our difficulties and bring glory to Him.

But if our only understanding of peace was the world's definition, then we would miss God's answer and lesson for us because we would be looking for something else, thus preventing God's peace from ruling in our hearts. Since we would probably conclude that God did not answer our prayer, we might become upset, perhaps even bitter against the God we claimed to have "faith" in.

It is easy to become disheartened in our prayer life if we are looking for results from the world's perspective. That's why we must not evaluate spiritual acts and responses with secular definitions.

As we take our first look at the evidences of a love relationship with the Lord and view how joy and peace are powerfully affected by that relationship, let's first explore the biblical usage of both joy and peace. Perhaps this study will encourage us to rethink our understanding of God's ways apart from the world's view, thus allowing us to experience a deeper love relationship with Him.

JOY

An acquaintance of mine approached me one day and said, "You know, Pastor, you must be happy, because you've always got a smile on your face." I responded, "Must I have a smile on my face to be happy?" "Well, no," he said, "But you wouldn't really have a smile on your face if you didn't have anything to be happy about."

His comments provoked me to rethink a few things in my life regarding my inner feelings and my outward appearance—especially since I felt I had developed a love relationship with God. This love relationship had certainly strengthened my joy in Him, but as a Christian, I knew joy was a special attribute reserved for Christians, since it is one of the fruits of the Spirit. Perhaps that was why I was constantly on guard with a smile in order to indicate to others that I was "happy," and that I was experiencing the fruits of the Spirit in my life.

But could this kind of approach cause other people to misunderstand what biblical joy really is? Is joy in the Lord nothing more than a smile on a Christian's face? How does a believer exhibit joyful characteristics that will set apart his joy in the Lord from a person's happiness in the world?

Most of us, if asked to explain the biblical concept of joy, might have difficulty clearly defining it. Yet Scripture presents a distinct, vastly different meaning from the world's definition of joy, which is simply happiness.

In the New Testament, the Greek word for joy is *chara,* which means delight. It is associated with hope and life, but the experiences of sorrow also prepare for and enlarge the capacity for joy.[1] In the world, happiness and unhappiness cannot exist together. But joy and sorrow can exist together. Jesus told His disciples that their sorrow would be turned to joy: "Truly, truly, I say to you, that you will weep and lament, but the world will rejoice; you will be sorrowful, but your sorrow will be turned to joy" (John 16:20). Jesus told His disciples that although they would mourn His death, their sorrow would be turned to joy upon His resurrection. Jesus used the analogy of a woman giving birth to a child (John 16:21). During the process of birth, there is much pain and agony. But after the birth, the pain and agony are turned to joy at the sight of the newborn child. Sorrowful experiences enlarge the capacity for joy when they are viewed in terms of their results.

There are three essential biblical features of joy that separate it from the world's "happiness":

- Joy is eternal.
- Joy is only for the believer.
- Joy is a state of mind not dependent on circumstances.

(1) *Joy is eternal.* Romans 14:17 declares, "The kingdom of God is not eating and drinking, but righteousness and peace and joy in the Holy Spirit." Joy is an eternal aspect of the Kingdom of God, for it is a part of the nature of the Holy

Spirit. It is an attribute of Deity (Psalm 104:31). As believers, we have Christ living in us. Through Jesus Christ, we have the promise of eternal life. This fact brings us to our next point.

(2) *Joy is reserved for the believer.* As Christians, we are indwelt by the Holy Spirit. The fruits of the Spirit listed in Galatians 5:22-23 are specifically for the believer: "The fruit of the Spirit is love, joy, peace, patience, kindness, goodness, faithfulness, gentleness, self-control; against such things there is no law." An unbeliever may manifest semblances of these spiritual fruits, but he cannot experience what believers experience. Apart from the indwelling Holy Spirit, true joy cannot exist. It has its own esoteric meaning rightfully owned and operated by our Lord for the purpose of serving, sustaining, and assisting the lives of those who serve Him. It exists for our encouragement, regardless of the circumstances.

(3) *Joy is a state of mind not dependent on circumstances.* Whereas happiness depends largely on happenings, good health, and so on, joy is inherent within the Christian life (the indwelling of the Holy Spirit). Paul said, "Now may the God of hope fill you with all joy and peace in believing, that you may abound in hope by the power of the Holy Spirit" (Romans 15:13). The fullness of joy and peace is based on the title "God of hope." Only the hope created by God gives a reason for joy and peace. When this hope is present, joy and peace will be made full.

The fullness of joy and peace gives a hope that abounds more and more in the hearts of those who harbor it. A key word in Romans 15:13 is "fill." The Greek word is *plēroō*, which means "to make full, to fill to the full." In the passive voice, it means "to be filled, made full." Thus, to be filled with all joy is a condition or a result to be continuously performed, regardless of our particular circumstances or situation. Our joy can be enhanced through our actions (John 15:11) or through a deeper love relationship (Psalm 5:11). But our joy is primarily the result of the hope of Christ living in us, not the result of our present feelings or circumstances.

In both the Old Testament and the New Testament, God Himself is the ground and object of the believer's joy. Psalm 35:9 states, "My soul shall rejoice in the LORD; it shall exult in His salvation." Psalm 43:4 says, "I will go to the altar of God, to God my exceeding joy; and upon the lyre I shall praise Thee, O God, my God."

Paul declared, "Rejoice in the Lord always; again I will say, rejoice!" God is the object of the believer's joy. The object of happiness, on the other hand, is the pleasure it provides. It can only manifest itself in the pleasant feelings of a given situation.

It is important for us to view the sources of biblical joy. Our understanding of these sources will further separate our definitions of joy and happiness. There are four sources:

- Our faith
- Our hope
- The joy of other believers
- Persecution for Christ's sake

(1) *Our faith*—Faith is our first source of joy. Our faith in a God of hope produces joy and peace (Romans 15:13). Therefore, our joy in the Lord is enhanced by our faith in the Lord. Paul said, "I know that I shall remain and continue with you all for your progress and joy in the faith" (Philippians 1:25). Here Paul was telling the Philippians that their lives in Christ should not be static, but rather characterized by an increasing amount of spiritual truth,

which would gradually deepen their joy in the Lord. Hence, the greater the faith (Romans 15:13), the greater the joy, since faith is a source of joy.

(2) *Our hope*—Paul spoke of the connection between hope and joy in Romans 5:1-2:

> Therefore having been justified by faith, we have peace with God through our Lord Jesus Christ, through whom also we have obtained our introduction by faith into this grace in which we stand; and we exult in hope of the glory of God.

The object of our rejoicing is our hope of the glory of God. This glorying state of mind takes place in the present, but it is something to be realized in the future. This future attainment is brought into relation with the present by hope. Our hope is the glory of God.

The glory of God can be viewed within at least two New Testament teachings: the manifestation of God's own glory, and the conforming of the believer to the image of the glory of Christ that will be revealed (1 John 3:2). Thus, our glory is based in our hope of the glory of God to come.

(3) *The joy of other believers*—Paul stated clearly in Romans 12:15, "Rejoice with those who rejoice, and weep with those who weep." This joy is not some kind of "happiness" we may feel with another person. Rather, it arises from our fulfillment and satisfaction in the Lord. Our challenge is to rejoice (be joyful) as if the situation of other believers were our own.

Even Christians sometimes have a tendency to envy or even despise a person who is in the thick of God's blessings. I am convinced that the deeper our love for God, the greater our capacity for joy, thus lessening our potential for envying those who are rejoicing.

(4) *Persecution for Christ's sake*—Jesus relates our joy to the persecution we suffer for His sake:

> "Blessed are you when men revile you, and persecute you, and say all kinds of evil against you falsely, on account of Me.
>
> "Rejoice, and be glad, for your reward in heaven is great, for so they persecuted the prophets who were before you." (Matthew 5:11-12)

Jesus here instructs us to rejoice greatly for three reasons: (a) persecution is often an indication of the genuine character of faith (the prophets, who were of godly character, were persecuted); (b) Christian character is purged and made mature through a degree of suffering (Romans 5:3,5; James 1:3-5); and (c) persecution is followed by a reward in heaven—not by any human merit, but by the grace of God.

Peter summarized these points in his first letter to Christians scattered during Nero's persecutions:

> Beloved, do not be surprised at the fiery ordeal among you, which comes upon you for your testing, as though some strange thing were happening to you; but to the degree that you share the sufferings of Christ, keep on rejoicing; so that also at the revelation of His glory, you may rejoice with exultation. (1 Peter 4:12-13)

PEACE

Probably my favorite word in the English language is "peace." For me, it communicates a certain gentleness and calmness—sitting alone beside a cool mountain stream in a time of prayer and conversation with the Lord.

Perhaps most people today would define peace as

simply the absence of war, or the elimination of hostile acts. After all, this is the primary dictionary definition.

In the New Testament, the Greek word for peace is *eirēnē,* which means binding "together that which has been separated."[2] Its counterpart in the Old Testament is *shalom,* which primarily signifies "wholeness."[3]

Throughout the Bible, peace is used in a variety of ways: a form of greeting (Nehemiah 6:15, Isaiah 42:19), an indication of freedom from outside hardships and internal distresses (1 Kings 4:24, Acts 9:31), and a description of concord between nations (Luke 14:32). It is also a term connoting peace within a nation (Acts 24:2), in churches (1 Corinthians 14:33), between people in general (Romans 14:19), and as a state of rest and contentment (Mark 5:34, Luke 2:29).

There are two further meanings in the New Testament that appear to be similar, but upon closer reading, we can see that they are very different and thus require clarification, especially as they relate to the love relationship. These two kinds of peace are (1) peace with God, and (2) the peace of God.

There is a significant difference between having peace with God and having the peace of God in our lives. Peace with God arises out of our faith in the knowledge that we are secure and justified with God, resulting from our willful acceptance of Christ's atoning work at the Cross (Romans 5:1,8,11; Colossians 1:20). The peace of God is for those who are already at peace with God. It is a resting confidence in the Lord resulting from our willingness to commit our anxiety, fears, and burdens in prayer and thanksgiving to Him (Philippians 4:7). Also, because of our obedience to God, His peace acts as a sentry, guarding our hearts from discouraging thoughts of anxiety and insecurity (John 15:10-11, 19:27; Colossians 3:15).

Kenneth Wuest notes certain differences between peace with God and the peace of God. Here are some of his very interesting comparisons:

> The first [peace with God] has to do with justification, the second [the peace of God] with sanctification. The first is the result of a legal standing, the second, the result of the work of the Holy Spirit. The first is static, never fluctuates, the second changes from hour to hour. The first, every Christian has, the second, every Christian may have.[4]

Thus, it is the peace of God that is enhanced through a closer walk with Him. It is the peace of God that is maintained and strengthened through a love relationship.

Therefore, our love relationship with God will, through His peace, guard our hearts against thoughts of anxiety, fear, and despair. This is not to say that such thoughts will no longer enter our lives. Rather, their control over our lives will decrease as the peace of God replaces such thoughts by ruling the seat of our emotions: our heart.

> Be anxious for nothing, but in everything by prayer and supplication with thanksgiving let your requests be made known to God. And the peace of God, which surpasses all comprehension, shall guard your hearts and your minds in Christ Jesus. (Philippians 4:6-7)

This is certainly one of the most profound promises God has given to believers. It is God's declaration to us to rest in Him. It is His way of providing an outlet for our anxiety and discouragement through the ministry of the Holy Spirit: "Now may the God of hope fill you with all joy and peace in believing, that you may abound in hope by the power of the Holy Spirit" (Romans 15:13).

After spending time in prayer with God, I always feel a sense of peace and calmness in my life. Whatever had troubled me before prayer never seems as urgent or pressing after prayer. It is as if the Lord takes a divine container full of peace and gently pours it over my life, washing away the needless pains of worry and distress.

At our church, the men get together every Tuesday for prayer before work. It has become a highlight of the week for all of us. Together we praise the Lord and worship Him through our prayers. It is especially exciting to see God move in situations that seem impossible to us. But perhaps the most immediate result of our prayer time is the peace of God that filters through our lives to prepare us for the day to come. The peace of God simply allows us to keep His love and grace in perspective, preventing the things of this world from influencing or disrupting us.

I often think of David and his responses to the many different crises he experienced throughout his life. One crisis in particular relates to the peace of God David experienced through his love, devotion, and prayer. David had just escaped from the Philistines, who had captured him. He had faked being a madman, knowing that the Philistines would release him rather than kill him. He hid in the cave of Adullam with four hundred men who were disillusioned, in despair, and in debt. In the midst of all this, David wrote Psalm 34, a psalm of praise. A few of its verses certainly characterize David's tremendous love for God, and the peace he experienced in trusting Him:

> I will extol the LORD at all times;
>   his praise will always be on my lips.
> My soul will boast in the LORD;
>   let the afflicted hear and rejoice.

Glorify the LORD with me;
    let us exalt his name together.
I sought the LORD, and he answered me;
    he delivered me from all my fears.

                             (Psalm 34:1-4, NIV)

As a result of giving his problems to the Lord in prayer, David felt neither anxiety nor fear, but experienced the peace of God, which strengthened him. Even though God did not specifically remove the problem (David was still hiding in the cave with 400 disgruntled men), David was able to endure—even to praise his God. Isaiah 26:3-4 reiterates David's psalm: "Thou wilt keep the nation of steadfast purpose in perfect peace, because it trusts in Thee. Trust in the LORD forever, for in GOD the LORD, we have an everlasting Rock." The peace of God is a result of our love and trust in Him.

JOY AND PEACE IN THE LOVE RELATIONSHIP

Truly loving the Lord will produce joy and peace, because both are fruits of the Spirit inherent within the life of every believer (Galatians 5:22). A believer, therefore, has the capacity to exhibit joy and peace as a result of his position in Christ. But the key issue is the extent to which these virtues—joy and peace—have control over a believer's life. To the degree that our bond with the Lord grows ever closer through our love relationship, His joy and peace will win control over our lives.

Winning control simply means that joy and peace become dominant personality traits within our character. In other words, because Christ is living in us, His joy and peace cause us to live our lives in a way that other people can clearly observe. We exhibit a strength in our Christian life, regardless of the conditions or circumstances.

Rejoicing in the Lord is a form of loving and adoring Him. Through the practice of praise and adoration, we grow stronger in Him. His joy becomes our joy, which is our spiritual strength (Nehemiah 8:10). But when our love for God weakens, so does our joy in Him. Thus, since the joy of the Lord is our ongoing source of strength, when our joy in God decreases, so does our strength to endure for Him.

Thus, our joy in the Lord is important to the longevity of our spiritual strength. This has often been overlooked by certain Christians who concentrate on legalistic activities to enhance or strengthen their spiritual condition. They have yet to see the importance in rejoicing in the God of Creation. They allow themselves only a semblance of praise in what they do or do not do. When the disciples gathered around the risen Christ just before His ascension into heaven, they honored Him for who He was: "They worshiped [Jesus] and returned to Jerusalem with great joy" (Luke 24:52, NIV). They were acknowledging Him as God and rejoicing in their worship of Him.

In His second farewell discourse, Jesus began to instruct the disciples about peace: "Peace I leave with you; My peace I give to you; not as the world gives, do I give to you. Let not your heart be troubled, nor let it be fearful" (John 14:27).

The peace Jesus spoke of was not peace with God, but the peace of God—the gentle, trusting confidence believers have available to them. It was not the peace of the world, which is a false peace, a peace that evolves from self-dependence or ignorance of impending doom. After giving the disciples His peace, our Lord said not to be troubled or fearful. Why? Because "the peace of God, which surpasses all comprehension, shall guard your hearts and your minds in Christ Jesus" (Philippians 4:7). Also, he who abides in God, abides in love, and there is no fear in love (1 John

4:16-18). Thus, to be in love with God means that we are abiding in Him and that fear has no control over us, for His peace is guarding our hearts and minds.

Much has been written about the apostle Paul. But perhaps the greatest feature about Paul's life was his divinely inspired ability to be content in the most difficult circumstances. He was a man totally in love with God. His love for God produced an extraordinary amount of joy and peace, which resulted in complete contentment in Christ.

After Paul was told by the prophet Agabus that he would be bound in Jerusalem, the Christians at Caesarea, along with those in Paul's group, begged him not to go to Jerusalem. But Paul, in love with his God and at peace with God's plan for him, responded, "'What are you doing, weeping and breaking my heart? For I am ready not only to be bound, but even to die at Jerusalem for the name of the Lord Jesus.' And since he would not be persuaded, we fell silent, remarking, 'The will of the Lord be done!'" (Acts 21:13-14).

After his arrest and his subsequent defenses before Felix, Festus, and Agrippa, Paul was put on a ship with 276 other men to sail for Italy. In the course of the voyage, they were caught in a violent storm, which caused the men to fear for their lives. Again, Paul, exhibiting the peace of God, encouraged the men to keep up their courage. He told them not to fear because God had told him that He would deliver them. Paul trusted totally in the Lord. He said, "I believe God, that it will turn out exactly as I have been told" (Acts 27:25).

From a prison cell, Paul, through the inspiration of the Holy Spirit, penned perhaps the greatest book on joy: Philippians. Throughout its contents, the joy of the Lord in Paul's life rings out loud and clear. Despite being chained in a prison cell, the apostle said without hesitation, "Rejoice in the Lord always; again I will say, rejoice!" (Philippians 4:4). Paul was certainly a living testimony of God's joy and peace to all who came in contact with him.

Knowing believers who exhibit such joy and peace has always been a tremendous source of encouragement to me. It renews my own joy and peace, especially when I have become preoccupied with problems or events of the day. It also strengthens my walk with the Lord and my fellowship with other believers. Moreover, it causes me to stop and reflect on the Cross of Christ, our sole reason for true joy and peace.

Since coming to Colorado a few years ago, Janet and I have had the privilege of entering into several close friendships with some families in our church. One such family has become very dear to us. In fact, we have an agreement to care for their children in the event that God should call both of them home. Terry and Trudy Thomson are true examples of believers who exhibit a fresh and enthusiastic sense of God's joy and peace. In conversation, you do not need to talk very long with them before you realize their deep love and commitment to God. Their lives are preoccupied with the love of God.

Yet within their family and ministry, they face as much, if not more, turmoil than most of us. But you would never know it by observing their lives on a daily basis. Why? Because the joy and peace of God are in control of them. The intensity of their love for God has punctuated every aspect of their lives, causing them to live each day in complete and total confidence in their position in Christ. Thus, in their contentment in Christ, they can endure all things through the joy and peace of God (Philippians 4:11,13).

Joy and peace are clear evidences of a love relationship with God. If it is a struggle for you to live in His joy and peace, you may consider evaluating the depth of your love.

Or perhaps you have never really applied your heart toward truly experiencing the joy and peace of God that He has intended for you. Whatever the case, the joy and peace of God, as evidences of the love relationship, should be a very important part of the life and spiritual growth of *every* believer. They must not be casually overlooked.

Let us remember Paul's exhortation to the church at Philippi:

> It is God who is at work in you, both to will and to work for His good pleasure. Do all things without grumbling or disputing; that you may prove your-selves to be blameless and innocent, children of God above reproach in the midst of a crooked and per-verse generation, among whom you appear as lights in the world, holding fast the word of life, so that in the day of Christ I may have cause to glory because I did not run in vain nor toil in vain. But even if I am being poured out as a drink offering upon the sacri-fice and service of your faith, I rejoice and share my joy with you all. And you too, I urge you, rejoice in the same way and share your joy with me. (Philippians 2:13-18)

NOTES:
1. W.E. Vine, *An Expository Dictionary of New Testament Words*, Volume 2 (Old Tappan: Fleming H. Revell, 1966), page 279.
2. Kenneth S. Wuest, *Word Studies*, Volume 1, page 131.
3. Vine, *Expository Dictionary*, Volume 3, page 170.
4. Wuest, *Word Studies*, Volume 1, page 76.

CHAPTER EIGHT

Endurance

*Those who love deeply never grow
old; they may die of old age, but
they die young.*
ARTHUR WING PINERO

Chained in a prison cell in Rome, Paul awaited his execution. He longed to see his "son" Timothy, and was cold and physically hurting. He wanted Timothy to bring him his coat, which he had left in Troas. He also wanted parchment to write on and some books to study. He knew that his end was near.

Detailing some of his requests and final salutations, Paul wrote a very personal letter addressed to Timothy and to the church at Ephesus. In this short epistle of 2 Timothy, the man of contentment and endurance urged his spiritual son to continue strong in the faith and to be an honorable servant of Christ. He also reminded Timothy of the importance of enduring persecution and suffering for the sake of the gospel. Perhaps the key verse is 2 Timothy 1:13: "Retain the standard of sound words which you have heard from me, in the faith and love which are in Christ Jesus."

It is not surprising that Paul tied the idea of endurance with faith and love in Jesus Christ. Paul had learned from his previous missionary journeys that endurance in Christ is directly related to a believer's ability to be strong in the faith by his unshakable love for God (Acts 15:36-40; 2 Corinthians 6:4-6, 12:10).

In many Christian circles today, there seems to be a large number of anemic Christians floating from church to church, hoping to find a better pastor or Bible study that will make them spiritually strong. But the key to spiritual strength is not so much who teaches us or what group we attend. After all, there are many believers who sit week after week under strong and powerful teaching who are still weak and brittle, with little endurance. The key is how we view God. Do we love Him enough to draw near to Him and trust totally in His guidance? Can we accept without complaint God's sovereign ways? Can we endure the trials of our belief merely on the fact of who God is?

The whole idea of endurance in the Christian life rests squarely on the strength of our love for the Lord! For it is by our love that we can be accepting rather than questioning, growing rather than backsliding, enduring rather than drifting. Only a love relationship with God establishes an enduring heart. This is the powerful message Paul was trying to get across to Timothy in this final epistle.

The word "endurance" brings to mind different pictures of strength, anguish, and fulfillment. It is also a word of respect, reflecting a positive quality in a person's character. The dictionary defines endurance as the "ability to last; to continue; to bear or tolerate pain and discomfort without flinching, quitting or letting down.'"[1] Most of us like to think that we possess endurance, that we are durable people in the face of trials. But endurance is a relative term if it is not put to the test and measured by consistent standards.

Athletic competition clearly displays one's ability to endure in measurable terms. Running a marathon (26 miles, 385 yards) in a certain amount of time indicates a degree of endurance. The one who finishes with the quickest time has, among other things, a greater ability to endure. But perhaps one of the greatest examples of endurance in the world of athletic competition is long-distance professional cycling. Road races are run consecutively over a period of days or weeks, which can drain a rider of all of his or her emotional and physical energy. Watching these riders battle the elements of the terrain and weather, the pain of continual physical exertion, and the mental strain of intense competition is a lesson in endurance.

Without a doubt, the greatest of these cycling events in the world is the *Tour de France*. It is an event that sometimes stretches over twenty-four days and covering over 2,500 miles. The riders follow a course outlining the country of France, from the flatlands of Brittany to the mountains of the Pyrenees and the Alps. Each day of competition involves from three to eight hours of racing and has its own unique course, from shortened time trials to lengthy hill climbs. This incredibly demanding event is considered by many to be the most remarkable example of physical and mental endurance in all of athletic competition.

One of its recent winners and the first American to ever win the Tour was Greg LeMond. His amazing conditioning and stamina allowed him to endure to victory in the 1986 Tour, which has been considered the most demanding Tour in recent memory.

I recall the intense drama that unfolded as LeMond

battled Frenchman Bernard Hinault for first place. Hinault was the hometown favorite competing on his own soil. He had already won the Tour five previous times. LeMond not only had to battle Hinault, but also the European press, which grinned when LeMond said the year before that he thought he could win the Tour. But driven on by his insatiable desire to win, LeMond endured to victory.

Watching this race on television, I was reminded of the illustrations Paul used about enduring through hardships in 2 Timothy 2. There Paul described the professions of soldier, athlete, and farmer. Interestingly, he does this directly after exhorting Timothy, "Be strong in the grace that is in Christ Jesus" (2 Timothy 2:1).

We must remember the example of the soldier. He lays aside all outside entanglements to focus his entire attention on warfare in order to endure on to victory in battle. The Christian life is essentially warfare against the forces of evil. If we are going to compete and endure through this warfare, we must be reminded of the soldier's example.

We must also remember the athlete. He would not dare to enter competition without first physically and mentally preparing himself. Like the professional cyclist who has trained for months and perhaps years for competition, we must constantly follow a rigid set of rules designed to guide us through our course in life so that we may be victorious after competing according to the rules.

And we should never forget the example of the farmer: "The hard-working farmer ought to be the first to receive his share of the crops" (2 Timothy 2:6). The emphasis in this verse is on the term "hard-working." Through his hard work, the farmer strives ahead in his labor to harvest a successful crop.

The bottom line of Paul's illustrations is relating the endurance and requirements of these professions to that which is required of the Christian who suffers the hardships of persecution in an unbelieving world. "Endure hardship with us like a good soldier of Christ Jesus" (2 Timothy 2:3, NIV), declares Paul. It is for the grace of God that we endure (2 Timothy 2:1).

ENDURANCE IN THE CHRISTIAN LIFE

The word "endure" corresponds with the Greek word *hupomenō,* which literally means "to remain under."[2] In the New Testament it refers to preserving something while under trials, and holding on to one's faith in Christ[3] (Luke 8:15, Romans 5:3, Hebrews 12:2). *Hupomonē,* the noun form of this word, is translated "patience" in several places (1 Corinthians 13:7; 2 Timothy 2:10,12; Hebrews 10:36, 12:2; James 5:11), but is much more of an active word than that. William Barclay points out that *hupomonē* is not the patience that passively endures. Instead, it is the quality that enables a man to stand on his feet facing the storm.[4] Barclay further describes this word:

> *Hupomonē* is not simply the ability to bear things; it is the ability to turn them to greatness and to glory. The thing which amazed the heathen in the centuries of persecution was that the martyrs did not die grimly, they died singing. One smiled in the flames; they asked him what he found to smile at there. "I saw the glory of God," he said, "and was glad." *Hupomonē* is the quality which makes a man able, not simply to suffer things, but to vanquish them. The effect of testing rightly borne is strength to bear still more and to conquer in still harder battles.[5]

Endurance in the Christian life is a key principle for spiritual stamina and growth. It is the quality that enables the believer to acknowledge the Lord through the most difficult of circumstances. A believer's endurance in Christ serves as a trophy of God's grace and power to the unbelieving world. It is the powerful symbol of God's promise that He will see the Christian through temptations by providing a way of escape, thus allowing him the ability to endure and stand firm (1 Corinthians 10:13, 2 Peter 2:9).

For the believer, what are the specific purposes of endurance? How can we develop endurance in the Christian life? How does endurance affect our spirituality? Moreover, how does endurance become a mark of our love relationship with God?

First, let us gain an understanding of its general use. Whenever endurance is spoken of in the New Testament, it generally refers to trials and testings that originate from outside circumstances. That is, it points to trials and testings that come by way of the world, impacting the life of the believer. These trials put a person's faith to the test. If his faith is genuine, it will develop endurance.

There are also some specific purposes of endurance in the life of the believer. They are found in the first chapter of James:

> Consider it all joy, my brethren, when you encounter various trials; knowing that the testing of your faith produces endurance. And let endurance have its perfect result, that you may be perfect and complete, lacking in nothing. (James 1:2-4)

From this passage, we can observe three specific purposes for endurance in the Christian life: It serves to discipline us; it helps to mature us; and it seeks to complete us.

(1) *Endurance serves to discipline us.* In Hebrews 12:7 we read, "Endure hardship as discipline; God is treating you as

sons. For what son is not disciplined by his father?" (NIV). In this verse, "discipline" refers to God's chastisement of believers, which is intended to develop our efficiency or self-control in a certain area of our lives. If we are to strengthen our control over problem areas, then we must endure the hardships God allows in our lives for that purpose. Hence, in our endurance we become disciplined (Hebrews 12:3-11, James 1:4). Our faith in Christ becomes a disciplined act of our will, having been tested and found worthy, steadfast, and immovable. And the whole process is reason to be joyful! (James 1:2).

God treats us as sons and daughters when He disciplines us, for this discipline builds up our faith. A recent situation involving my son illustrates this point.

At the end of our family room sits a wood stove upon a raised brick platform. Ever since his first steps, Ryan has been fascinated with the wood stove. At first he tried several times to touch it, even while it was hot. Janet and I then spent about a week's time teaching him never to touch the stove, whether it was operating or not. After the week of training, we felt that Ryan finally understood our discipline. But one day, Ryan slipped away to take a swipe at the stove while it was operating. We grabbed him just as his fingers brushed the side of the stove, but it was a second too late. He slightly burned three of his fingers, which, of course, provoked a loud cry.

Ever since this incident, Ryan has seemed to place more trust in our training. He has developed a certain amount of faith in our instruction, perhaps realizing our instruction is in his best interest.

This is similar to our relationship with God. As our love for Him increases, so does our capacity to endure hardships, because our faith and trust in Him rests in the knowledge that He will always do what is in our best interest, as well as His (Romans 8:28, 1 Peter 1:5-9). Unfortunately, most of us must learn this lesson through experience. God must bring us through His "fatherly discipline" so that we learn to depend on His love and faithfulness. But in this lesson, we gain a greater capacity for endurance, which develops our discipline, allowing us to share in His holiness (Hebrews 12:11).

(2) *Endurance helps to mature us spiritually.* "Perseverance [endurance] must finish its work so that you may be mature and complete, not lacking anything" (James 1:4, NIV). James is saying here that our endurance has a job to do. Its job is to bring us to maturity. The only way this is accomplished is by our endurance *through* our trials and hardships (Romans 5:3-4). Thus, growing in our ability to endure quickens our development toward spiritual maturity.

I recently heard an illustration of a brother and sister who were climbing a large hill together. The hillside was covered with large boulders, which made climbing difficult. About halfway up the side of the hill, the sister stopped and complained about all the rocks and boulders they had to climb on. Her brother stopped her and responded, "These boulders are here for a purpose: to help us get to the top." The boy was quite perceptive in his response. He understood that the purpose of the boulders was to help them endure the difficulty of climbing on them. He did not allow the trials at hand to cause him to lose sight of his goal of reaching the top.

Spiritual maturity is, in many respects, like climbing a mountain. At the start, you intensely contemplate the climb. There is a bit of apprehension as you think of all the possible complications along the way. The summit is not fully in sight, which adds a degree of awe or anxiety. But because it's the early morning and you have prepared yourself mentally, you are ready and willing to endure the climb.

As the day proceeds, fatigue begins to set in. Your legs become weak and your feet are sore. You start to slow down and may even entertain thoughts of quitting and turning back. But every now and then along the trial, you catch a closer glimpse of the summit, reminding you of your commitment to reach it. The thought pumps encouragement into you. Soon, other climbers around you begin to complain about the hardships and some of them even decide they don't want to go any farther. But because you are serious about your climb and have made a personal commitment to reach the top, your determination is strong enough to motivate you to overcome the physical and mental obstacles.

Interestingly, as you get closer to the top, the hardships of the climb become less threatening, less annoying. Your thoughts of reaching that pinnacle begin to replace the pain and hardships of the climb. A renewed spirit of energy replaces the pain in your body. Your endurance grows stronger and stronger as you near the summit.

Experienced mountain climbers say there is an imaginary point separating the serious climber from the casual climber. It is a point that occurs just after the first difficult section has been successfully climbed. It is at this point where thoughts of quitting are in the minds of almost all climbers. It is the point of no return, a point that symbolically launches the climber toward the summit without thoughts of quitting. Only the serious climber, who is by determination thoroughly committed to reaching the top, will press on after this point.

This is referred to as the point of confidence. Overcoming the suggestion to quit gives confidence to the climber to reach the summit. He then has the right attitude to endure hardships he will face during the rest of the climb.

Physical and mental endurance are necessary attributes not only for the serious climber but also for the person who wants to achieve spiritual maturity. Our endurance despite the suggestions of quitting and the temptations of sin is a key factor in our ability to climb the mountain of spiritual maturity. Endurance indicates obedience. God's character is revealed to us as we rely faithfully and obediently on Him.

Paul understood this process of spiritual maturity. After declaring that his great desire was to know God, Paul referred to his endurance, his continual *pressing on* for the knowledge of God according to his upward call:

> Brethren, I do not regard myself as having laid hold of it yet; but one thing I do: forgetting what lies behind and reaching forward to what lies ahead. I press on toward the goal for the prize of the upward call of God in Christ Jesus. (Philippians 3:13-14)

Paul understood that the climb toward spiritual maturity was a continuing responsibility. He was also well aware that our endurance in the climb is a necessary factor in our process of maturing in Christ.

(3) *Endurance seeks to complete us.* The concept of completion in James 1:2-4 does not refer to our perfection. Rather, it points out the fact that the nature of endurance causes us to lack nothing. Endurance is one of the most important virtues we can have as believers to help present us before the Lord spiritually mature (Hebrews 12:1-2,5-11; James 1:4). It is that all-encompassing trait that will survive anything the world forces on us. It is the one complete quality helping us "run . . . the race that is set before us, fixing our eyes on Jesus the author and perfecter of faith" (Hebrews 12:1-2). Endurance is the ability to continue in our faith by resisting the pressure of the world (Luke 8:15).

It is always a comfort to learn of other people who have faithfully endured through difficult situations. James reminds his readers of the endurance of Job and the prophets of God, who maintained their witness while living through tremendous persecution and personal tragedy:

> As an example, brethren, of suffering and patience, take the prophets who spoke in the name of the Lord. Behold, we count those blessed who endured. You have heard of the endurance of Job and have seen the outcome of the Lord's dealings, that the Lord is full of compassion and is merciful. (James 5:10-11)

No doubt James also had in mind something he stated earlier, which relates our endurance to *hope*:

> Blessed is a man who perseveres under trial; for once he has been approved, he will receive the crown of life, which the Lord has promised to those who love Him. (James 1:12)

All of this leads us to conclude that through endurance we develop godly character. This character assures us of sharing in the divine glory of God (Romans 5:3-5), because our faith in Him is proven in the process of godly discipline. The testing God allows in our lives serves to build our trust and faith in Him. If we do not really believe in God, we will not endure through the difficult tests. Thus, our endurance becomes a clear mark of our love for God. And in our endurance, we grow spiritually.

DEVELOPING ENDURANCE

Before we stand up and declare to God and the world that we will forever exhibit steadfast endurance, we must first understand the process of developing that endurance. It does not just descend upon us overnight. It must be learned through faith and experience.

Endurance is difficult to learn because it often involves pain, either emotional or physical. The only way it can be learned is by an act of our will. We need to be powerfully motivated to choose to endure a certain trial or conflict. As believers, our motivation to endure in the Christian life should and must be out of our sincere love for God (Mark 12:28-30).

For example, say a person has a great love for riding in an airplane. He is fascinated by everything associated with flying: the planes, the high speed, and the act of flying itself. But in order to experience flying in closer detail, he decides to take flying lessons. The training soon becomes long and arduous. But because of this person's intense love for flying, his motivation to learn gives him a tremendous amount of endurance to continue through the rigors of training.

Likewise, in our pursuit to draw nearer to God, our motivation to truly love Him causes us to endure the trials and persecutions along the way. But how do we train our will to learn endurance? It must come through a process of rigorous emotional and spiritual training. Athletes must continually train and condition their bodies to perform to optimum level in competition. Christians, too, must train and condition their emotional and spiritual endurance for the persecutions and trials that will come.

Involved in this training are three basic principles to learn and understand: the difference between good and evil; walking by faith, not by sight; and the temporary nature of our afflictions and the constant renewal of our inner spiritual life.

(1) *The difference between good and evil*—Christians need to be on guard not to become lazy in their walk toward

spiritual growth. The author of Hebrews makes an interesting comparison between the immature believer and the mature believer. The immature believer is constantly occupied with "the elementary principles of the oracles of God" (Hebrews 5:12). He remains on milk rather than advancing to solid food.[6] The mature believer, on the other hand, takes in solid food: the deeper, more advanced instruction in the truths of God.

"Because of practice," mature believers "have their senses trained to discern good and evil" (Hebrews 5:14). In other words, as a result of training, the eater of solid food (the mature Christian) is constantly exercising himself in spiritual perception. Thus, he does not run the risk of doing the wrong thing when trials and difficulties enter his life. His maturity in Christ is stronger because his ability to discern good from evil has boosted his endurance through external difficulties.

Many times I have seen an immature believer face a difficult situation and make a wrong decision because he lacked the discernment to choose between what was best for him in the long run and what looked like the easiest way out. In his haste to ease the pain or pressure, he chooses what he feels is the quickest way out, never really contemplating the possibility that facing the trial would be in his best interest. Consequently, he never learns endurance because his first thought is always to escape.

In many ways, this is similar to the case of a child who has told a lie. When confronted, he takes the easiest way out and denies it to avoid the punishment. And as long as the child continues to get away with finding the easiest, least incriminating avenue out of his problems, he will never learn responsibility, endurance, or discipline.

We all need to learn and remember that what we *think* is good may not be what is good for us from God's perspec-

162 / Evidences of a Love Relationship

tive. We can gain this understanding from the practice of training our senses in the "solid food" of God's truths: that is, learning about and knowing God from quality time alone with Him and the study of His Word (2 Timothy 2:15, 3:16).

(2) *To walk by faith, not by sight*—In a discussion on the difficulties he encountered in spreading the good news of the gospel of Jesus Christ, Paul encouraged the believers at Corinth to remember that they would again be united with Christ in glorified bodies. They had to trust in this truth, not by what they saw, but by faith—"for we walk by faith, not by sight" (2 Corinthians 5:7).

A believer can know that the Lord is present, not by what he sees, but by faith. When difficulties arise, however, the immature believer tends to lose sight of this truth by trusting first in himself. He has not learned how to truly walk by faith in God, because he has not yet committed himself in total dependence to God. Thus, endurance is never realized because when the chips are down, he only trusts in what he sees, not in the faith he has confessed.

But by our faith in Christ, "We know that in all things God works for the good of those who love him" (Romans 8:28, NIV). We learn endurance as we go through difficulties trusting in Him.

I know a particular young man who took several years to learn this truth. Being very independent at the time of his conversion, it was difficult for John to learn to walk by faith in Christ and not by his own sight. Thus, his maturity in Christ was a slow process. Because his endurance was weak, he unknowingly drifted from Christ whenever a new trial entered his life. When John would finally come to the end of himself in his search for solutions, he would then turn to the Lord and make a new commitment. But soon he would lapse into the same independent condition as before. Then after a major trial, he would again come to the end of his rope and turn to the Lord.

John came to me a number of times while he was immersed in these struggles, asking me how he could become a stronger Christian. Even though he spent a lot of time reading his Bible (he even taught a Bible study), he just couldn't figure out why he struggled so much with living the Christian life. Finally, after nine years as a struggling Christian, John saw through the quagmire to the penetrating reality. While he was listening to a message on Paul's admonition to walk by faith and not by sight, John finally understood how a Christian can truly endure for the Lord in trials. He learned that walking totally by faith will give him the right perspective of God's sovereign power and grace, thus strengthening his will to endure.

Interestingly, John's conclusions bring us full circle, back to the truth we learned from James: The testing of our faith produces endurance (James 1:3). Learning to walk by faith and not by sight is indeed a test in itself, but it is also a disciplined act of our will motivated by our love for God. Let us also not forget that "without faith it is impossible to please Him, for he who comes to God must believe that He is, and that He is a rewarder of those who seek Him" (Hebrews 11:6).

(3) *The temporary nature of our afflictions and the constant renewal of our inner spiritual life*—Persecution and affliction are only temporary, not eternal. And though our physical bodies are decaying, our inner spiritual life is constantly being renewed. If we truly understand this principle, we should be able to develop true spiritual endurance.

Persecution and affliction were daily occurrences for the apostle Paul. But he was able to develop endurance through it all because (a) he knew it was only temporary (2 Corinthians 4:17), (b) he knew that its end result would be resurrection with Jesus Christ (2 Corinthians 4:14), and

(c) he knew that his inner spiritual life was being renewed day by day (2 Corinthians 4:16).

If we knew and understood these reasons, we, too, would certainly develop a steadfast endurance in all our difficulties. But many of us, despite our "faith" in Christ, are still preoccupied about the here and now and our personal well-being. So, while in the midst of trials, we are unable to direct our thoughts toward anything else but our escape from the pressing circumstances of the moment.

Peter adds another interesting feature to our endurance in hardships. He points out that if we patiently endure hardships for Jesus' sake, in doing so we will find favor with God. Peter was relating this fact to the Christian domestic servant of his day, but it is very applicable for us today:

> For this finds favor, if for the sake of conscience toward God a man bears up under sorrows when suffering unjustly. For what credit is there if, when you sin and are harshly treated, you endure it with patience? But if when you do what is right and suffer for it, this finds favor with God. (1 Peter 2:19-20)

Peter is focusing here on those trials and sufferings that occur to us because of our stand as believers in Jesus Christ, not on those trials and sufferings resulting from our sin and disobedience. We find favor with the Lord when we endure sufferings as a result of doing what is right in His eyes. God is so creative that He is able to use all forms of trials and sufferings, whether to glorify Himself, to discipline us, or to bring us to repentance.

* * *

Understanding these three basic principles in the process of learning endurance will help us develop a steadfast, immovable endurance in Christ, which will shine to all the world as a trophy of our love for God. There have been thousands of Christians down through the centuries whose endurance for Christ through extreme sufferings—even those leading to death—has shined to many in their generation. As a result of their faithful example, many have been won to Jesus Christ.

I remember in my early college days, just prior to my conversion, reading about Christian martyrs and how they sacrificed everything, including their lives, for the sake of Jesus Christ. I remember thinking to myself what tremendous love and faith these people must have had in their God. He must have been a powerful reality in their lives in order for them to endure the way they did.

Reading about many of these people was one of the contributing factors to my conversion. The stories of their valiant courage and commitment in the face of death forced me to do some serious thinking. The fact that so many people put their lives on the line for what they believed in indicated that they must have truly experienced God's reality and love through Jesus Christ. No phony mystical experience or myth could have ever motivated them to endure the atrocities they encountered.

The stories of two of these early Christians made an indelible mark on my thinking: the apostle Andrew and a twenty-six-year-old woman named Perpetua. Both of these committed believers displayed an enormous amount of endurance in the heat of persecution and suffering. Their stand for the Lord Jesus Christ eventually led to their martyrdom.

Andrew—Though his name never appeared first on a list of disciples, Andrew was the first one to follow Jesus. His older brother Peter was always listed first. In fact, that was the way it was at home ever since their childhood days. Peter was always getting the attention, while Andrew was growing up in his shadow.

It's never any fun to grow up in the background of someone else. But that was Andrew's position in life. Peter was always in the spotlight, while Andrew was quietly behind the scenes doing his job without complaint. Interestingly, even Scripture treats Andrew with a degree of indifference. Three of the four times his name appears, it is followed with the clarification, "Simon Peter's brother"! Perhaps when we get to heaven, Andrew will introduce himself to us as Simon Peter's brother.

Yet this shy young man was the first to respond to Christ through the teachings of John the Baptist (John 1:35-40). It was Andrew who brought Peter to Jesus, saying, "We have found the Messiah" (John 1:41-42). We read about Andrew only four times in the Gospels. Each time, he is bringing someone to Jesus. The first time he brought himself (John 1:40); the second time he brought Peter (John 1:42); the third time he brought the little boy with five barley loaves and two fish at the feeding of the five thousand (John 6:8-10); and the fourth time he and Philip directed some visitors from Greece to Jesus (John 12:20-23). Andrew was a young man who may not have had the great preaching ability to draw thousands to Christ, but he did have a quiet, friendly spirit that attracted individuals.

H.S. Vigeveno's commentary on Andrew is very true to life:

We remember the Peters, but we forget [the] Andrews. They write no stirring epistles. They preach no great, great sermons. They do not win three thousand with one message. They work no miracles. But they bring the Peters who write the epistles, who preach the sermons, who win the three thousand, who work the miracles in men. . . . But Jesus chose Andrew. He chose him first. Why? Because one-talent people are indispensable to the Kingdom. Nothing can be done without those friendly folk, those humble people, who are always introducing others to Jesus.[7]

This humble servant of God was one of the men who "turned the world upside down" (Acts 17:6, KJV). Out of Andrew's intense love for God, he endured much persecution and suffering while spreading the gospel to many Asiatic nations.

Andrew's martyrdom was a testimony of his courage and faithfulness. Tradition has it that while in Edessa, he was preaching against the idols worshiped in that country. Egeas, the governor of the country, ordered that Andrew be taken and tied by a rope to an X-shaped cross.

For two days while hanging on the cross, Andrew continued to tell others about Jesus Christ. During those two days, he won so many people to Christ, that the people rushed the governor's chamber demanding that Egeas release Andrew. Fearing a riot by the people, the orders were given to cut Andrew down. But as the last cord was cut, Andrew fell over and died. It was said that he prayed the following just before his death:

> O Jesus Christ, let not thine adversary loose him that is hung upon thy grace; O Father let not this small one humble any more him that hath known thy greatness. But do thou, Jesus Christ whom I have seen, whom I hold, whom I love, in whom I am and shall be, receive me in peace into thine everlasting tabernacles, that by my going out, there may be an entering in into thee of many that are akin to me, and that they may rest in thy majesty.[8]

How could a man endure such suffering? Only out of a deep, intense love for his God. Tradition goes on to relate that in Andrew's endurance, he "more glorified the Lord" through his death.[9]

Perpetua—After the second century, persecutions of Christians extended into Africa. Perpetua's martyrdom was perhaps the most renowned. Her incredible story of courage, faithfulness, and endurance through sufferings and trials was a powerful example of God's reality in a believer's life.

At the tender age of twenty-six, Perpetua was seized for being a Christian and thrown into prison, even though she was a wife and mother with an infant. Her father went to her cell in an attempt to persuade her to renounce Christianity. When she refused, her father became so angry that he severely beat her. Still, she and a few other believers together with her in prison continued to rejoice in the Lord and were later baptized.

She was then taken before the proconsul Minutius, who demanded that she sacrifice to idols. When she refused, she was ordered to be placed in a dark dungeon, separated from her child. She gladly accepted her sentence, realizing that she must leave everything for Christ's sake. She said to her father at his second visit, "God's will must be done."[10]

An historian relates this information about her second and final trial:

Perpetua gave the strongest proof of fortitude and strength of mind in her trial. The judge entreated her to consider her father's tears, her infant's helplessness, and her own life; but triumphing over all the sentiments of nature, she forgot the thought of both mental and corporeal pain, and determined to sacri-

fice all the feelings of human sensibility to that
immortality offered by Christ. In vain did they attempt
to persuade her that their offers were gentle, and her
own religion otherwise.[11]

Perpetua endured the most difficult suffering of all:
separation from her newborn child, rendering her infant
helpless. As new parents, Janet and I cannot think of anything more painful than to be separated from our son. Yet
Perpetua stood firm in her faithfulness to God. She did not
waver! Perpetua was later executed with several other Christians by being thrown to wild beasts and stabbed by an
executioner's sword.

* * *

The examples of Andrew and Perpetua may sound horrid
to our generation and culture, but they are all the more
powerful when you stop to think about what they endured.
Surely no one with a weak love for Christ would have stood
so strong in the face of such atrocities. Only a deep love
could have caused a believer to stand so courageously.

But what about us today? Are we to believe that the only
way to prove our love for God is for us to endure suffering to
the point of death? No, not at all. But there are still situations, even today, where Christians are threatened with
prison sentences, even torture and death, for their stand in
Christ. Most of us need to be reminded of what the author
of Hebrews says about enduring sufferings:

Consider Him who has endured such hostility by
sinners against Himself, so that you may not grow
weary and lose heart. You have not yet resisted to the
point of shedding blood, in your striving against sin;
and you have forgotten the exhortation which is

addressed to you as sons, "My son, do not regard lightly the discipline of the Lord, nor faint when you are reproved by Him; for those whom the Lord loves He disciplines, and He scourges every son whom He receives." (Hebrews 12:3-6)

May we never forget the example of Christ. May we always be reminded of His example of love and endurance for the Father. And let us not forget that in our trials, God is communicating His love to us by making us strong and proven. So let us show our love to Him by our endurance. Let us not weaken in persecution and trial. And let us remember the encouraging words from Paul, who truly understood the hidden advantages of suffering and persecution:

Let us not lose heart in doing good, for in due time we shall reap if we do not grow weary. (Galatians 6:9)

NOTES:

1. *Webster's New World Dictionary* (New York: Merriam, 1975), page 203.
2. Wuest, *Hebrews,* Volume 2, page 218.
3. Wuest, *2 Timothy,* page 133.
4. Gaebelein, ed., *The Expositor's Bible Commentary,* Volume 12, page 168.
5. William Barclay, *The Letters of James and Peter* (Philadelphia: Westminster Press, 1976), page 43.
6. Milk and solid food are used as metaphors for the truths of God. "Milk" refers to elementary truths and "solid food" refers to the deeper, more advanced truths.
7. H.S. Vigeveno, *13 Men Who Changed the World* (Ventura: Regal Books, 1986), pages 15-16.
8. Herbert Lockyer, *Last Words of Saints and Sinners* (Grand Rapids: Kregel Publications, 1975), pages 44-45.
9. Lockyer, *Last Words,* page 45.
10. John Foxe, *Foxe's Book of Martyrs* (Old Tappan: Fleming H. Revell, 1979), page 20.
11. Foxe, *Foxe's Book of Martyrs,* page 20.

CHAPTER NINE

Worship

*Come, let us worship and bow
down; let us kneel before the
LORD our Maker. For He is
our God, and we are the people
of His pasture, and the sheep of
His hand.*
PSALM 95:6-7

"What is true worship?" a professor asked his class of young
Bible students. After a moment of silence, a shy young man
stood and said, "I think I know, but it's a little difficult for me
to explain. Before I was a Christian, I used to dislike going
to church. I was always late and hardly ever attentive. Now,
as a Christian, I love to go early to sit quietly and think about
God and His great love for me!" Then with tearful eyes he
said, "I love Him more than anything in this world because
He chose to love me while I was a sinner. Now all I want to
do is please Him, and to know Him as deeply as I can."

This young man understood worship. Because of his
deep love for God, his only motivation was to give honor

and glory to God through his obedience and praise. He is an example of the people Peter referred to as "God's own possession": "You are a chosen race, a royal priesthood, a holy nation, a people for God's own possession, that you may proclaim the excellencies of Him who has called you out of darkness into His marvelous light" (1 Peter 2:9).

I firmly believe that worship is one of the ingredients sorely lacking in Christianity today due to the fact that our love for the Lord simply lacks depth. It is in many circumstances only a surface love, a love that is not deep or intense enough to motivate us to invest the necessary time and energy to sincerely worship Him.

When our love is weak, our response to God is also weak, such as worshiping only on Sunday. We lack the desire to sit daily with the Lord and do as David recommends in Psalm 29:1-2: "Ascribe to the LORD, O sons of the mighty, ascribe to the LORD glory and strength. Ascribe to the LORD the glory due to His name; worship the LORD in holy array."[1]

We in the twentieth century have developed a fast-food spiritual mentality. Because of our busy schedules and our narrow understanding of how to love and worship God, we quickly go before the Lord in prayer (which is the only form of worship we say we have time for) and we don't really worship Him at all. All we do is ask Him for this or that. We then expect His blessings to immediately fall upon us with as little of our own sacrifice as possible. When we don't get quick results or the answers we expected, we become impatient and frustrated. We then lose any interest in praising or worshiping Him because we feel He has let us down.

The problem here is that we have missed the point of our existence. God was not created for us, but we were created exclusively for Him! (1 Corinthians 8:6). As Peter said, we are God's *possession.* Thus we are to proclaim *His* excellence. Nowhere in the Bible does it indicate that it is God's duty to proclaim our excellence and to meet all of our desires. If we are not truly living for Him, then our desires will not be His desires. The emphasis throughout the Word of God is always on what we as believers can be to Him: to give Him praise and glory from our hearts, honor and obedience in our actions. With that kind of relationship, we can freely say with Job in times of disappointment, "Naked I came from my mother's womb, and naked I shall return there. The LORD gave and the LORD has taken away. Blessed be the name of the LORD" (Job 1:21).

For several years after I became a Christian, I had a narrow understanding of what worship really involved. I had gained a limited perception of its meaning from church services and occasional devotionals, but I never fully realized what worship really was. To me, worship was simply a duty accomplished by attending the church worship service every Sunday morning. The worship took place in reading Scripture, singing hymns, giving offerings, and listening to sermons. These were certainly the proper forms of worship. But because I had become accustomed to a routine, I did not gain the deeper reality of truly worshiping the Lord from my heart. Worship had become an obligation to *do,* not an expression of grateful reverence.

Not until I began to develop my love relationship with the Lord did I realize that my understanding of worship was very limited. As I grew in love with God, my worship of Him through devotion, praise, adoration, and thanksgiving became an active response from my heart, expressing itself in many creative ways. Many of the praise psalms of David began to come alive to me. And my awareness of God became more of a reality throughout my life as I more deeply sensed His presence in my daily walk.

Worship for me today is a powerful element of my

spiritual life. Whether in the traditional, formalistic worship service, or in a more free service with clapping of hands, I can thoroughly enjoy the Lord in worship of Him because my deeper love for Him has changed my motivation and attitude. Both my personal worship of God and my worship with other believers are now far more edifying to my Christian life (1 Corinthians 14:26).

Worship serves to remind me of God's awesomeness, uniqueness, and faithfulness. It also serves to humbly remind me of my position in Christ: How fortunate I am to be counted among His children! What a waste of positive spiritual energy and enthusiasm when a believer mistakenly approaches the worship of God as an obligation or as a play in which the actors come together and perform their weekly ritual out of conscience's sake.

DEFINING WORSHIP

The word "worship" comes from the old Anglo-Saxon word "worthship." The primary New Testament word for worship is *proskuneō,* which denotes the act of bowing or prostrating oneself in submissive lowliness and deep reverence (Matthew 4:10, John 4:21-24, Revelation 4:10). Though Scripture nowhere gives a clear definition of worship, we may draw its meaning from passages that describe its character and our response (1 Chronicles 16:29; Psalm 2:11; Isaiah 12:5-6; Matthew 2:2; Luke 4:8; Philippians 2:10, 3:3; Revelation 4:10-11).

By definition, true worship is the sincere expression of devotion to God. It is an inward experience that seeks to comprehend the reality of God through Jesus Christ. W.E. Vine further clarifies that worship is not confined to praise, but can be "broadly . . . regarded as the direct acknowledgment to God, of His nature, attributes, ways and claims, whether by the outgoing of the heart in praise and thanksgiving or by deeds done in such acknowledgment."[2]

Worship in Old Testament times meant a sacrifice of some sort to God—burnt offering, sin offering, or peace offering, for example. In order to be acceptable to God, these offerings had to be accompanied by a sincere heart. A person's heart had to manifest itself in outward obedience to God's laws (Isaiah 1:10, Hosea 6:6, Amos 5:12). We know that genuine worship involved the inner experience, for praise and prayer were considered the primary part of the sacrifice (Psalm 51:17, 69:30).[3]

Worship for us today no longer requires an offering of an animal or some grain. Rather, it is the offering of ourselves to God, acknowledging His presence in our lives through our devotion, praise, adoration, and thanksgiving. Paul describes this as our reasonable service:

> I urge you therefore, brethren, by the mercies of God, to present your bodies a living and holy sacrifice, acceptable to God, which is your spiritual [*logikos*—reasonable] service of worship. (Romans 12:1)

We further have the New Testament revelation that we worship God in spirit and in truth (John 4:24). The spirit and truth are closely related and seen in the person of Jesus Christ. In his defense of the faith against false teachers, John accurately described the reality of knowing God as that of knowing the reality of Christ. It is through the Spirit of Christ that we worship God:

> We know that the Son of God has come, and has given us understanding, in order that we might know Him who is true, and we are in Him who is true, in His Son Jesus Christ. This is the true God and eternal life. (1 John 5:20)

Thus, within our union with Christ, we are able to "offer up spiritual sacrifices acceptable to God" (1 Peter 2:5). Since Christ is our mediator, He is our link with the Father in all prayer, which is a form of worship. Thus, we pray in the name of Jesus (John 16:23-26) and worship God—through Christ—in spirit and in truth.

THE PRACTICE OF WORSHIP

Richard Clarke Cabot said that worship renews the spirit as sleep renews the body. I think the analogy is accurate, especially in regard to our need for spiritual regularity. Just as our body requires sleep on a regular basis to renew its strength and to help maintain its health, our spirit requires a daily time of worship and devotion to the Father to renew its strength and to help keep us from drifting in the Christian life. If we do not worship on a regular basis, our sensitivity to the things of God may begin to weaken as temporal responsibilities attempt to preoccupy us. Our worship of the Lord is in many respects a measure of our commitment. And our commitment is founded in consistency.

Although the New Testament does not outline for us an ideal program of worship, we can recognize at least six different *forms* of the church worship service. These are (1) preaching (Acts 20:7); (2) the reading of Scripture (1 Timothy 4:13); (3) prayer (Acts 2:42, 1 Timothy 2:8); (4) singing, praise, and thanksgiving (Ephesians 5, Colossians 3:16); (5) baptism and the Lord's Supper (Acts 2:41, 1 Corinthians 11); and (6) giving (1 Corinthians 16:1-2).[4]

Note that these forms do not illustrate a particular *style* of worship. There is a difference between *forms* of worship and *styles* of worship. Forms of worship are avenues of different methods that aid a believer in recognizing the awesomeness of God and helping him draw nearer to Him. Styles of worship (which can be creative and many in number, such as clapping hands or not clapping hands, raising hands or not raising hands, and so on) are the different activities that accentuate a particular form in order to enrich the worship experience for the believer.

Different styles of worship result from personal or denominational preferences. An important point to remember here is that while one style of worship may accentuate a particular form of worship for one believer, it is not necessarily more spiritual than another style. The issue in worship styles is not so much the style, but the awareness or impression of the greatness of God it creates in the believer. So, if it serves as an aid in drawing the believer nearer to God in an unconfused, biblical manner, then it is proper for that particular believer.

But we should be cautioned against extreme styles from both ends. The ultra-fundamental, formalistic approach could become entangled in legalistic do's and don'ts, which may quench the Holy Spirit and prevent the Lord from soliciting responses from the hearts of people in worship. Then at the other end, too much of an expressive emotional display could, in fact, hinder the worship experience by causing one to lose sight of the object of his worship—the Lord—because he may become overtaken by the experience itself.

In any event, it would not be edifying to the Body of Christ for any believer to declare his church's particular style of worship as any better than another's. God has created all of us to be unique and individual. That is why He has allowed different denominations. What style may serve one group of believers may not serve the needs of another. We must always remember that what we do for the Lord is for His glory and not for our personal glorification or recognition. "Whether, then, you eat or drink or whatever you do, do all to the glory of God" (1 Corinthians 10:31).

THE LOVE RELATIONSHIP AND PRIVATE WORSHIP

Up to this point we have mostly considered various worship forms and styles. Also, in previous chapters we have viewed how a love relationship with God will change our attitude about spending time with Him. Because of the in-love relationship, our time with Him is never out of duty or obligation. It comes from a sincere response of the heart to His love and care for us. Consequently, our worship within an assembly of other believers can always be powerful and edifying regardless of the particular form or style. Because our love for God is the focal point of our worship, the form or style implemented to aid our worship is not so critical.

But perhaps the love relationship has its greatest effect in our quiet times alone with God when we ascribe our worship and devotion to Him. I believe there are at least two reasons for this that deserve our attention and understanding.

First, a deep, genuine love for God will motivate our hearts and minds to search out and create more personal opportunities beyond public worship, causing us to draw nearer to Him in the worship He desires. In doing this, we are showing God that we seek to be His worshipers.

The Greek word "seek" in John 4:23 is *zēteō*. It describes exactly what God is looking for in believers. He is seeking Christians who know how to worship Him in spirit and truth. Notice the context in which this word is used in John 4:19-24:

> The woman said to Him, "Sir, I perceive that You are a prophet. Our fathers worshiped in this mountain; and you people say that in Jerusalem is the place where men ought to worship."
>
> Jesus said to her, "Woman, believe Me, an hour is coming when neither in this mountain, nor in Jerusa-

lem, shall you worship the Father. You worship that
which you do not know; we worship that which we
know; for salvation is from the Jews. But an hour is
coming, and now is, when the true worshipers shall
worship the Father in spirit and truth; for such people
the Father seeks to be His worshipers. God is spirit;
and those who worship Him must worship in spirit
and truth."

This was our Lord's response to a woman who tried to
involve Him in an ongoing controversy about where worship should take place. For many years there had been
sharp disagreement between the Jews and the Samaritans
whether worship should be offered in Jerusalem, where
Solomon's Temple had been built, or on Mount Gerizim,
where Jesus was speaking to this woman.

The Samaritans claimed that when Moses instructed
the people about their entrance to the Promised Land, he
commanded that an altar be set up on Mount Ebal. Then
the twelve tribes were divided: half to Mount Gerizim and
half to Mount Ebal. The Samaritans believed that the tribes
on Gerizim received the blessings of God and the tribes on
Ebal received the curses of God (Deuteronomy 27:1-15,
28:1-15).

The Jews, on the other hand, believed that Jerusalem
should be the center of worship since that was where
Solomon had been commissioned to build the Temple
(1 Kings 6).

In His answer to the woman, Jesus avoided the controversy by going right to the heart of the matter. He
declared that God was not interested in the location or
place of worship, but rather that people worship in spirit
and in truth. Then Jesus qualified the importance of this
kind of worship by saying that the heavenly Father *seeks*

those kinds of worshipers.

Interestingly, nowhere in Scripture does it say that God seeks something else other than people who know how to worship Him! What a profound thought! God is searching for men and women who can truly commune with Him through worship in spirit and in truth.

To worship God in spirit and in truth means involving yourself with the Lord in a close relationship through an open and honest heart. Because God is a spirit, He is not a material being that can be confined to one place. Thus, our worship of Him cannot be confined to any one place or to any one way. It should be expressed from the heart—the seat of our emotions.

A Christian who is experiencing a love relationship with the Lord will be the kind of worshiper God seeks, because he worships God freely—without a feeling of duty, from the very depths of his being. He is always looking for new and creative ways to give praise, glory, adoration, and thanksgiving to God. He doesn't expect anything in return from God except His approval. If God chooses to bless in various ways, then so be it. But if He chooses not to, that's okay, too, because true love does not expect anything in return. Worshiping the Lord in spirit and in truth is, indeed, a precious byproduct of the love relationship.

Second, the private response of true worship to God is initiated out of a genuine, heartfelt desire. This sincere desire is not motivated by any ulterior motive, such as trying to look pious before our fellowman. Rather, it is only motivated by an intrinsic desire to please God. In other words, our public worship may earn us recognition from man, but our private worship earns us recognition from God alone. After all, in private worship no one is there to pat us on the back to tell us how spiritual we are. The Pharisees were very adept at publicly displaying their ritual "worship" of God.

That's why our Lord referred to Pharisees as "hypocrites." But God loves our private worship because He knows that our hearts have been prompted to worship by Him alone.

God's response is similar to what our response would be toward a person who has fallen in love with us. Would we rather have someone love us because of what our relationship would contribute to his or her life—popularity or affluence, for example? Or would we prefer someone loving us for no apparent reason other than who we are as a person? It does not demand much reasoning to understand the heart of God in this light.

If we deeply love the Lord, we will surely want to set aside some time every day to go to the Father in worship, not just on Sunday morning. We can worship in the privacy of our own thoughts in our own room, or with other believers—it doesn't matter. The Lord is not impressed with ceremony, but with worship from a humble, loyal servant whose only desire is to draw near to the very nerve center of God Almighty. God seeks such believers to be His worshipers.

HINDRANCES TO WORSHIP

In our discussion of worship, we would be negligent if we did not observe some hindrances to our worship. Scripture alludes to a few certain instances in which negative behavior or actions will hinder our worship of God. While it is true our love relationship with God enhances our worship experience, the fact that we still bear a sin nature and struggle in the flesh demands that we be cautioned of the hindrances. To be forewarned is to be forearmed.

A good friend of mine was aggressively pursuing a deeper worship experience with the Lord. His love for God was growing stronger and his desire to draw nearer to Him was sincere. After a couple of months of trying various activities to aid his worship, Rick came to me in frustration, saying that he was unable to feel a genuine sense of worship. There just seemed to be something lacking, and he couldn't put his finger on it. He was also finding it difficult to concentrate and felt restless during his quiet times.

Well, feeling restless and having difficulty concentrating during a quiet time are not necessarily spiritual problems resulting from a negative action or behavior. There have certainly been times when I have felt restless and unable to concentrate because I was physically tired or mentally pressured. But for this to occur time and time again may suggest a spiritual problem. Rick was experiencing this frustration far too often. His feeling that something was wrong with his worship suggested to me that together we should probe for something hindering his worship to God.

It turned out that there was something in Rick's life that had been hanging over him for almost a year. Several years before, his father divorced his mother. It was a very painful experience for Rick, one that had a profound effect on his life. Because Rick felt that the divorce was his father's fault, he held a personal grudge against him. Later his father became a Christian and repented of his actions. But Rick was unable to forgive him and continued to carry the grudge.

All of us, at times, carry within us a certain amount of unresolved conflict that can affect us emotionally but not necessarily hinder our worship. But in Rick's case, he had been totally unwilling to forgive his father even after his father asked his son's forgiveness. When all of this surfaced in our discussion, Rick finally realized that his sin of unforgiveness toward his father was probably affecting his worship. He knew that he needed to deal with the unforgiveness in order to have a clear conscience before God *and* before man.

It took several weeks of prayer and resolution for Rick to finally go to his father and tell him that he forgave him, as well as to ask his father's forgiveness for carrying the grudge. As soon as he did this, not only did he renew a strong relationship with his earthly father, but he also began to experience a deeper intimacy in worship with his heavenly Father.

It's not surprising that in a growing love relationship with God, the closer we draw to Him, the more accepting we are when He reveals things that we need to deal with. This was the case with my friend Rick. The Lord used the worship experience to reveal an unforgiving spirit toward his father.

In terms of our worship, there are at least four different kinds of hindrances that not only hinder our worship but could also very easily hinder our progress in a love relationship with God.

(1) *Unconfessed sin*—The psalmist expresses very clearly God's response toward a believer who comes before Him with sin in his life: "If I regard wickedness [sin] in my heart, the Lord will not hear" (Psalm 66:18). Also, we break our fellowship with God when we have sin in our lives: "If we say that we have fellowship with Him and yet walk in the darkness, we lie and do not practice the truth" (1 John 1:6). If we do not enjoy fellowship with the Lord, surely we cannot expect Him to respond to our worship when our fellowship is broken.

Furthermore, how could we offer up ourselves in sacrifice through worship (Romans 12:1) when we are declaring our faith and loyalty from a heart shrouded in sin? If we attempt to do so, "We lie and do not practice the truth." In order to clear our worship, we must cleanse our lives from sin (1 John 1:9), thus restoring our fellowship with God.

(2) *Unforgiveness*—Failure to forgive is related to un-

confessed sin. God will not hear our confession of sin if we ourselves are not willing to forgive others:

> "Whenever you stand praying, forgive, if you have anything against anyone; so that your Father also who is in heaven may forgive you your transgressions. But if you do not forgive, neither will your Father who is in heaven forgive your transgressions." (Mark 11:25-26)

Jesus told Peter that we must be able to continually forgive. In other words, we should have a forgiving spirit (Matthew 18:21-22).

Unforgiveness despite sincere repentance is contrary to the nature of God, who is holy (Leviticus 11:44, 1 Peter 1:16), righteous (Deuteronomy 32:4, John 17:25), and merciful (Luke 6:36). Therefore, such unforgiveness must be humbly confessed to God and honestly resolved before our fellow man, in order to allow our worship to be acceptable to the Lord.

(3) *A self-centered or prideful spirit*—A self-centered spirit could be defined as an attitude of arrogance and selfishness that has its foundation in the wisdom of man (James 3:13-17). It is a form of pride that, by definition, means self-worship. James writes, "Whoever wishes to be a friend of the world makes himself an enemy of God. . . . God is opposed to the proud, but gives grace to the humble" (James 4:4,6).

From a worldly perspective, it would be very easy to view the worship of God as a "what's in it for me" experience. We give as long as we can get something in return. Such an attitude is not at all pleasing to God. It shows a complete misunderstanding of what true worship is.

We could also enter into worship with feelings of discontentment or impatience. But such negative feelings would indicate that we are not satisfied with God's design for our lives. Sincere worship could never evolve from such a mind-set.

Paul describes what our mind-set should be: "Set your mind on the things above, not on the things that are on earth" (Colossians 3:2). Let us especially observe Paul's counsel as we enter into worship with God.

(4) *Impurity*—Impurity is something that defiles a man from within, leading him to involve himself in impure acts. Here's how Jesus described it:

> "That which proceeds out of the man, that is what defiles the man. For from within, out of the heart of men, proceed the evil thoughts, fornications, thefts, murders, adulteries, deeds of coveting and wickedness, as well as deceit, sensuality, envy, slander, pride and foolishness. All these evil things proceed from within and defile the man." (Mark 7:20-23)

Paul states that it is the will of God for us to abstain from all sexual immorality to control our passions "in sanctification and honor" (1 Thessalonians 4:3-5). If we cannot, we are essentially rejecting God:

> For God has not called us for the purpose of impurity, but in sanctification. Consequently, he who rejects this is not rejecting man but the God who gives His Holy Spirit to you. (1 Thessalonians 4:7-8)

If we desire to truly worship the Lord, then our hearts and minds must be free from impurity. Now, we are not necessarily impure if we experience a sudden reaction to an initial display or suggestion of something impure. The impurity comes in if our second reaction is not to reject the temptation and flee from it. Paul adamantly warned young Timothy, "Flee from youthful lusts, and pursue after righteousness, faith, love and peace, with those who call on the Lord from a pure heart" (2 Timothy 2:22-23).

The psalmist must have understood impurity and its results because he related it to a young man: a person who might be more susceptible to its evil, subtle ways. But the psalmist also provided the solution: "How can a young man keep his way pure? By keeping it according to Thy word" (Psalm 119:9).

If we can heed the warnings from Christ and the cautions and solutions from Paul and the psalmist, each of us can go before the Lord with an unblemished heart and a clear conscience, thereby insuring that our worship will be rich and meaningful both to us and to God.

* * *

In his first Epistle, Peter illuminated these four hindrances to worship in a passage where he characterized principles that should govern the Christian community. These principles should be reflected in the life of every Christian. This is our standard of behavior in approaching the Lord in worship:

> To sum up, let all be harmonious, sympathetic, brotherly, kind-hearted, and humble in spirit; not returning evil for evil, or insult for insult, but giving a blessing instead; for you were called for the very purpose that you might inherit a blessing. For "let him who means to love life and see good days refrain his tongue from evil and his lips from speaking guile. And let him turn away from evil and do good; let him seek peace and pursue it. For the eyes of the Lord are upon the right-

eous, and His ears attend to their prayer, but the face of the Lord is against those who do evil." (1 Peter 3:8-12)

The worship of God is an awesome and powerful experience. We must never enter into it with a flippant attitude or an insincere heart. Therefore, our aids to worship must be activities that cause us to focus totally on God. (For suggestions for aids to worship, see Chapter 5.)

When we have a rich love relationship with God, the worship experience becomes a direct means of our expression of adoration and devotion toward Him. It is our main avenue for communicating our warmest feelings, deepest thoughts, and utmost praise to the Creator of everything we know. It is our opportunity to draw near to the Holy of Holies, the Alpha and the Omega, the First and the Last, the Beginning and the End. What an incredible opportunity we have as finite beings to sense the reality of our infinite and holy Maker!

In the fourth chapter of the book of the Revelation, we read John's account of being taken to heaven and given a glimpse of the very throne of God and those who worship around it. John's moving and graphic description has always given me chills and caused me to stop in awe and humbly dwell on the supremacy and holiness of Almighty God. May I suggest that you read Revelation 4:1-11 slowly and try to visualize the scene as if you were there? This simple exercise can be a wonderful means for bringing us to that place of spontaneous and reverent exclamation of God's greatness where we worship Him by joining in the eternal chorus of His praise:

"Worthy art Thou, our Lord and our God, to receive glory and honor and power; for Thou didst create all things, and because of Thy will they existed, and were created." (Revelation 4:11)

NOTES:
1. "Holy array" most likely refers to the holiness of God. Thus, this verse could read, "Worship the Lord for the beauty of His holiness."
2. Vine, *Expository Dictionary*, Volume 3, page 236.
3. Robert L. Saucy, *The Church in God's Program* (Chicago: Moody Press, 1972), page 168.
4. For an excellent study in the forms of worship, I refer you to Robert L. Saucy's book (above), *The Church in God's Program*, pages 166-234.

CHAPTER TEN

Guidance

Every man's life is a plan of God.
HORACE BUSHNELL

I am always interested in reading polls and statistics about religion. They tend to reflect current trends and beliefs that are making their way through a cross section of the populace. I recently read the results of a religious survey taken by a well-known national news magazine.[1] The results were interesting to me because they pointed to the fact that most people—by far the majority—are very concerned about religious beliefs as well as the role of religion in their personal lives. For example, note some of its key results:

- 94 percent have read at least some part of the Bible.
- 20 percent read it every day.

- 96 percent believe in God (or the idea of a Supreme Being).
- 87 percent say religion is important to their lives.
- 73 percent consider themselves religious.
- 80 percent believe in heaven.
- 72 percent believe they are going to heaven.
- 90 percent believe that God knows everything.
- 93 percent believe God hears and answers their prayers.

After reading these statistics, one would expect a greater influence of religion in our culture than there really is today. But, of course, the term "religion" is a general term that can be applied to every object of worship, whether a Supreme Being, a tangible object, or an abstract principle.

But the survey did indicate some interesting conclusions about why religion plays such a major role in people's lives. The underlying factor seems to be *guidance.* People have a great need to believe in supernatural guidance in their decision making.

Religion sociologist Ted Long says, "It extends beyond Sunday morning and past church doors. We make decisions every day based on what religion has taught us is right and wrong."

For most, religion is the ritual that sees us through the passages of our lives. Claudia Faust, 32, an office worker, puts it this way: "Without God, I think we would be just like a pinball in a pinball machine—bouncing around without any real purpose in life." Experts say religion is so ingrained, it guides our lives subconsciously. Says Timothy Hynes [a Catholic Washington, D.C., artist who does not attend a church anymore], "I rarely think about religion or

God. I don't pray. But it's part of my operating struc-
ture. Subconsciously, it's how I make my decisions."[2]

Making decisions in many cases is a difficult process. There
is always the looming prospect that the decision will be
faulty. Perhaps the added confidence a person feels from
"checking" his decision with a higher authority is the primary reason why many seek supernatural guidance. This
would explain why so many people claim that religion plays
a significant role in their lives.

But even more interesting is the fact that according to
the survey, 87 percent of the people say that religion is
important to their lives, yet the survey further indicated that
only 45 percent attend weekly religious services.[3] These
results strongly suggest that most people want to rely on the
guidance of God, but do not want to give any more thought
or attention to Him apart from His guidance.

What about Christians? How does our involvement in a
love relationship with the Lord affect our guidance? Do we
involve ourselves in church out of a subconscious desire to
receive guidance from God as a reward for our faithfulness?
Or do we view guidance as an assumed result of our relationship with God and a part of His sovereign plan for our
lives?

Guidance has, indeed, become a source of controversy
and confusion. To one believer, the guidance of God is a
moment-by-moment revelation from Him determining our
every move. To another, guidance is relying on the truths in
the Word of God and then employing godly wisdom (based
on those truths) in making decisions in areas not specifically addressed in the Bible. To another, guidance comes in
the form of inner impressions and supernatural revelations, perhaps without any regard to previously revealed
truths in Scripture.

Guidance is a controversial subject because it is such an important matter to every believer. Accordingly, we seem to have a general fear about the whole subject, a fear that perhaps we could miss what God may want for us. I agree with J.I. Packer's observation that the fear many Christians have "is not that no guidance should be available for them, but that they may miss the guidance which God provides through some fault of their own."[4]

Certainly guidance is a very important aspect of our Christian walk. Because we desire to please God, we try to do what is pleasing to Him (Ephesians 5:8-10). What pleases Him is our obedience to His will, which in turn glorifies Him (Psalm 23:3).

In our discussion of guidance, we will observe how a closer walk with the Lord in a love relationship will motivate us to eagerly pursue His guidance for our lives. As we grow in our understanding of His desires, our own desires will be changed, enabling us to better recognize His guidance for us. But first, let us establish an understanding of His guidance.

UNDERSTANDING GUIDANCE

It must first be recognized that God indeed has a plan for every believer (Psalm 37:23; Romans 8:14,28; Ephesians 1:4). It is a shared belief among many conservative evangelical theologians that within God's guidance, there are at least two distinct features. These features form the basic concept of what we may refer to in general as the will of God.[5]

(1) *The sovereign will of God*—God determines or decrees what will happen, whether He wills it directly or permits it to occur through our actions. This is the sovereign will of God. It is by His sovereign will that God knows everything that has happened and everything that will

come to pass (Psalm 135:6, Proverbs 16:33, Daniel 4:35, Romans 11:33-36, Ephesians 1:11, Revelation 4:11). Also, His decrees of these activities are not revealed to us.

(2) *The moral will of God*—The moral will of God consists of His moral truths for our behavior, character, and purpose, revealed specifically to us in the Word of God (Romans 2:18, 12:2; Ephesians 5:15-18; 1 Thessalonians 4:3-4, 5:16-18; 2 Timothy 3:16; 1 Peter 2:12-15, 4:3-4; 2 Peter 3:9). These truths, if obeyed, allow us to conform more to His image and character, thereby allowing us the privilege of drawing near to Him and intimately knowing Him (2 Chronicles 15:2, Hebrews 7:18-19, James 4:8). As we draw nearer to Him, we learn more of His desires, which gives us a clearer perspective of His individual will for us. But because of sin, these moral truths can be misused or disobeyed.

The sovereign will of God is what will happen regardless of our actions. The moral will of God is made up of His moral truths that He wants us to learn and practice. But in the freedom that He has chosen to give us, we may choose to disobey His truths. (God's sovereign will may be referred to by others as His decretive, determined, or secret will. His moral will may be referred to as His desired, permissive, or revealed will.) We are always in God's sovereign will, but when it is said that we are "out of God's will," we have violated His moral will.

To help clarify these two features even further, let us consider a couple of examples. According to James 5:9, it is one of God's moral truths (hence, His moral will) that as a Christian, I should not complain against another brother in Christ. But after attending a church committee meeting in which a proposal I submitted for approval was heavily criticized by a certain member of the committee, I begin criticizing that member in conversation with others. By my criticism, I have disobeyed God's moral will to not complain (much less gossip) against another brother. Therefore, I commit sin and break my fellowship with God.

But it was in God's sovereign will that I was going to complain, even though it was my own choice to disobey His moral will. God is able to use this situation for His glory, because through the conviction of the Holy Spirit, I feel guilty for complaining and seek forgiveness. My fellowship with the Lord is then restored and I place myself back in His will. Thus I learn another lesson about His forgiveness and about one of my weaknesses.

It is God's moral will that we should not love the world because the love we have for the world will preclude the love we have for God (1 John 2:15). Well, I knew a young Christian man named Brad who had a problem with commitment. He was frustrated about being unsure of God's plan for him. But because he continued to have an appetite for activity in the world and acceptance by his peers, he chose to hold on to his old nonChristian friends. And they continued to influence him to attend worldly parties.

Brad was unable to let go because the things of the world were still very real, very attractive to him. And since his love for God was weak, his level of commitment was shallow, making it easier to disobey God's commandments. Because he had not spent much time reading and appropriating God's Word, perhaps he had not yet discovered, among other things, that friendship with the world is hostility toward God (James 4:4). Either way, regardless of whether or not he was knowledgeable of it, he was still guilty of disobeying the moral will of God. Consequently, the Lord did not hear his prayers for guidance (Psalm 66:18, Isaiah 58:9-11).

Later, after being arrested for driving under the influence of alcohol, he finally realized what he had to let go of.

He then repented of his errant ways and separated himself from his nonbelieving friends. Moreover, he reestablished his commitment to God as his number-one priority. By doing this, he placed himself back in fellowship and in the will of God. Now he was far more able to appropriate God's truths in his life, giving him a much better perspective on God's guidance for him.

The Lord was aware that Brad was going to choose his temporary path of unrighteousness, as well as his eventual repentance. The whole process falls into the category of God's sovereign will. But it was Brad's decision to violate one of God's moral truths, which resulted in sin and broken fellowship with God. Yet God still used the entire situation to bring glory to Himself by allowing Brad to see the folly of his ways and face the consequences of his sin through a difficult experience. And from that experience, he was able to repent and receive God's complete forgiveness.

In order to discover God's individual guidance for our lives, we must gain understanding of His moral truths revealed to us in His Word. God works within our personal, unique, and individual character. He permits us a certain amount of individual expression within His sovereign will. This "individual expression" is the allowance He makes to let us discover and make decisions consistent with His moral will. But when these decisions move us outside the parameters of His moral will, we are given warnings in several different ways: by the conviction of the Holy Spirit (John 16:8-11), through God's discipline (Hebrews 12:5-11), or even from a crisis (1 Corinthians 5:4-5, 11:29-32).

God's will may be revealed to us through His Word, godly counsel, answered prayer, or providential circumstances. His specific guidance may very well be related to an individual's unique character. Each of us has been created with unique talents, strengths, and gifts. Thus, is it not logical for His revealed truths to inspire each of us in an individual way, but in a similar direction? This similar direction is within His sovereign will, and our created uniqueness becomes the basis for individual guidance.

Therefore, we will not discover His individual guidance from mystical inward impressions or peculiar revelations derived from coincidence or hearsay, but rather from God's revealed truths (His moral will) in the Bible. Based on our own uniqueness, we respond to His truths by an individual response that He directs in those truths.

Isn't this the design of the Body of Christ? Are there not many different members but one Body? We trust Christ in our lives, then some of us become evangelists, pastors, teachers, helpers, and givers. God uses our individuality and uniqueness to inspire His individual will for us, and in our response to His moral truths, His individual plan is further revealed to us.

We can see God working like this in the lives of several biblical characters. Two immediately come to mind, one in the Old Testament and one in the New Testament.

Lot was a righteous man (2 Peter 2:8). But because of his greed and selfishness (Lot's unique and individual character), Lot made a wrong decision, which moved him out of the moral will of God (Genesis 13:5-10). He chose to enter the perverse city of Sodom and to sit down with the ungodly (Genesis 14:12).

It was within God's sovereign plan that Lot was going to place himself out of His moral will. Consequently, God saw fit to allow Lot to suffer loss. He lost everything: his wife, his wealth, his influence. Even his relatives mocked him (Genesis 19:17-28). God's individual plan for Lot was revealed through his individual character and his response to the moral truths of God.

The life of Peter reveals a similar pattern, but with a

different ending. The Bible reveals for us in vivid detail Peter's unique and individual character. He was proud, impulsive, rash, and often insensitive toward others. Yet he had an assertive boldness about him that made him a worthy disciple for the cause of Christ (though it also got him in trouble on some occasions).

When you read about Peter's life—his ups and downs, his strengths and weaknesses—you can see how God's individual plan for him developed as you view his unique character. He was the first to walk on water toward Jesus (Matthew 14:28-31); he was the one who rebuked our Lord when He told the disciples how He must suffer and be persecuted (Matthew 16:22); he was the one who announced to Jesus that he would never deny Him (Mark 14:29). Peter was proud and bold, always wanting to be first. This attitude gave rise to his major character flaw: He was shallow in his commitment to God, and the Lord knew it.

But within His sovereign will, God used Peter's individual character to bring glory to Himself and to make Peter an object lesson to all believers. When Peter lied and denied our Lord three times, he moved himself out of the moral will of God. He then suffered an emotional and spiritual crisis (Matthew 26:69-75). But through this experience, Peter discovered God's unique plan for him: to be faithful and devout in his love for God (John 21:15-17), and more specifically, to become one of the greatest leaders of the Church in his day (Acts 2 and 3).

It was in God's individual plan for Peter that he would be the way he was and do the things he did. God utilized Peter's unique character and His moral truths to reveal His will to him.

The moral guidance of God revealed in Scripture is certainly the key force for growth and stability in the believer's life (Colossians 1:9-10). It has to be, for it is the directional pointer of how we are to live our lives, and why. It also works to cause us to acknowledge God as the supreme and sovereign ruler in our lives, whose plan for us is a perfect plan, a plan we can trust in (Romans 12:2).

> Not merely does God will to guide us in the sense of showing us His way, that we may tread it; He wills also to guide us in the more fundamental sense of ensuring that, whatever happens, whatever mistakes we may make, we shall come safely home. Slippings and straying there will be, no doubt, but the everlasting arms are beneath us; we shall be caught, rescued, restored. This is God's promise; this is how good He is. Thus it appears that the right context for discussing guidance is one of confidence in the God who will not let us ruin our souls. Our concern, therefore, in this discussion should be more for His glory than for our security—for that is already taken care of.[6]

THE LOVE RELATIONSHIP AND GUIDANCE

We have already noted in previous chapters that falling in love with the Lord is an intrinsically motivating experience. With our heart and mind we choose to intimately love Him without any external inducements or reinforcements. We do so out of a sincere response in acknowledging who God is and what He has done: He is the God and Creator of everything that is known, who chose to show His love to us by sending "His only begotten Son" to die on the Cross for our sins (John 3:16).

In our understanding of guidance, we have observed that by the sovereign and moral features of God's will and through our individual and unique character, He chooses to individually guide us. Furthermore, His moral will is foundational to the growth and stability of every believer.

Now, since the moral truths of God are revealed in the Bible as commands for our behavior and purpose, then it should go without saying that by virtue of our intimate love for God, we will have a far greater desire to walk by His commands. This was a point Jesus made to His disciples:

> "He who has My commandments, and keeps them, he it is who loves Me; and he who loves Me shall be loved by My Father, and I will love him, and will disclose Myself to him." (John 14:21)

John reiterated the words of Jesus:

> By this we know that we have come to know Him, if we keep His commandments. The one who says, "I have come to know Him," and does not keep His commandments, is a liar, and the truth is not in him; but whoever keeps His word, in him the love of God has truly been perfected. By this we know that we are in Him: the one who says he abides in Him ought himself to walk in the same manner as He walked. (1 John 2:3-6)

In our desire to please God by our deeper love and faithfulness, we are motivated to further study Scripture in order to gain more understanding of the character of God and His revealed truths. With this wider knowledge, we gain more and more insight into His individual guidance for us as His truths become seasoned into a greater degree of personal godly wisdom. This, in turn, allows us a far greater opportunity to make decisions consistent with His moral will. God works His truths through our decisions and in our individual and unique character to reveal His individual guidance to us. It would be out of character with His overall sovereignty (Ephesians 1:7-8) and omniscience (Isaiah 46:9-10, Matthew 10:29-30) to do anything less (Psalm 48:14).

But the key to this whole process of individual guidance is the depth of our love for God! What else could possibly motivate us enough to continually press on to know God and discover His truths, and then appropriate those truths into our lives regardless of the costs? What else could possibly cause us to freely submit ourselves totally to His will for His glory, even though it may not be what we originally had in mind? If we are truly walking in a love relationship with God, then His desires will be our desires and we will become filled with the knowledge of His will. This was one of the points Paul stressed in his letter to the church at Colossae:

> We have not ceased to pray for you and to ask that you
> may be filled with the knowledge of His will in all
> spiritual wisdom and understanding, so that you may
> walk in a manner worthy of the Lord, to please Him
> in all respects, bearing fruit in every good work and
> increasing in the knowledge of God. (Colossians
> 1:9-10)

If, then, to be filled with the knowledge of God's will is to walk in a manner worthy of the Lord, then what better manner is there than to walk *in love* with the Lord? Paul stressed to the believers at Ephesus that they were to be "imitators of God, as beloved children, and walk in love" (Ephesians 5:1-2).

The believer who has chosen to involve himself in a love relationship with the Lord will not have as much concern or difficulty in trying to "locate" God's guidance for himself. It is not a matter of trying to locate God's guidance, but simply a matter of discovering it in His Word as He reveals it to us according to His sovereign plan and our response to His moral will.

LIVING HIS GUIDANCE IN LOVE

I used to think that living according to God's guidance was something I had to do or perform. After all, His moral truths, from what I could see, were simply commands for us to perform. But when I began to fully experience my love relationship with God, my understanding of His commands began to change. They were no longer commands to do or perform but truths I wanted to live or be. My love for God made me want to display my commitment to Him through my obedience to His truths.

There is a difference between what we do or perform and what we live or are. Doing or performing something implies a temporary act, perhaps done out of obligation or forced by some external circumstance. Such actions do not signify a consistent, life-changing reality.

Living or being implies a personality trait that has become an inseparable quality of an individual's life. Such qualities represent something habitual—a consistent pattern. They are character attributes that make an indelible mark in a person's life. Let's look at a New Testament truth for an example.

Five times in the New Testament we are told that if we humble ourselves, God will exalt us (Matthew 23:12; Luke 14:11, 18:14; James 4:10; 1 Peter 5:6). The humbling process is a moral truth of God. Now, if humbling ourselves is something that we must do or perform, then it cannot be a response from the heart. Rather, it becomes an obligation to do or a task to perform. Thus, our humility will most likely resemble a temporary change.

But in contrast, if we view "humble yourself" as something we must live or be, then our humility becomes an inseparable attribute that has taken root within us. It is a consistent character trait woven into our daily lives.

The New Testament alludes to at least seven specific principles that are directly commanded as the will of God (His moral guidance). These principles, when viewed in their proper context, clearly display commands that are to be *lived* (as a permanent trait) and not just performed (as a temporary change).

(1) *Be saved.*—"God . . . desires all men to be saved and to come to the knowledge of the truth" (1 Timothy 2:3-4; see also 2 Peter 3:9). It is the command or moral will of God that everyone should be saved. His individual guidance can begin only at this point. But, just as importantly, after our conversion we should live as people who are saved.

(2) *Be sanctified.*—Paul said, "This is the will of God, your sanctification; that is, that you abstain from sexual immorality; that each of you know how to possess his own vessel in sanctification and honor, not in lustful passion, like the Gentiles who do not know God" (1 Thessalonians 4:3-5). The scriptural command here is that our sanctification should not be something that we perform, but a lifestyle that we live out. The way we live should be consistent with what we believe. Thus, we must be set apart from sexual immorality by knowing how to handle our bodies in honor and glory to God.

(3) *Be joyful* (1 Thessalonians 5:16).

(4) *Be prayerful* (1 Thessalonians 5:17).

(5) *Be thankful.*—Paul said, "Rejoice always; pray without ceasing; in everything give thanks; for this is God's will for you in Christ Jesus" (1 Thessalonians 5:16-18). There are three commands in this passage. By our Christian testimony and from within our human personality, we should continually exhibit a joyful, prayerful, and thankful attitude.

Such an attitude will be absolutely receptive to God's moral truths, therefore making our outward obedience to His direction a glory to Him and an example to the people around us.

(6) *Be submissive.*—Peter offers us some counsel that is difficult for most of us to apply:

> Submit yourselves for the Lord's sake to every human institution: whether to a king as the one in authority; or to governors as sent by him for the punishment of evildoers and the praise of those who do right. For such is the will of God that by doing right you may silence the ignorance of foolish men. (1 Peter 2:13-15)

God commands us to submit to all human authorities as an active demonstration of our submission to Him. We should have a daily attitude of respect and reverence for God that manifests itself in a continual demeanor of subjecting ourselves to one another. This kind of active submission shows a willing heart that is totally yielded to the guidance of God.

(7) *Be willing to suffer.*—Peter said, "Let those also who suffer according to the will of God entrust their souls to a faithful Creator in doing what is right" (1 Peter 4:19). God wants us to live with a willingness to suffer for His sake. He may choose for us to encounter a greater amount of persecution than another believer suffers. If so, we must have a willing heart to endure the suffering for His glory.

Every one of these seven principles is something to *be,* not to perform. We are to live the commands of God's guidance, not just perform them. Walking in a love relationship with the Lord will cause a sincere believer to be motivated to walk in such a manner. He will understand the differences between performing and living, between doing and being. And when a Christian has such an understanding of God's will, the guidance of God becomes a far more immediate reality.

Many times I see teenagers struggle with their parents' authority. But as these youths grow and mature, many tend to develop a renewed sense of love and commitment toward their parents. Along with this revival of love is a renewed sense of trust in their parents' counsel and guidance. What is happening is similar to our relationship with God and His guidance. As our love for Him grows deeper, so does our trust and loyalty toward Him. Therefore, we become far more open and receptive to His guidance as He reveals it to us in His truths.

Certainly, as we develop our love relationship with the Guide, He is progressively equipping us to do His will, which is pleasing in His sight. Let us truly learn the benediction to the book of Hebrews:

> Now the God of peace, who brought up from the dead the great Shepherd of the sheep through the blood of the eternal covenant, even Jesus our Lord, equip you in every good thing to do His will, working in us that which is pleasing in His sight, through Jesus Christ; to whom be the glory forever and ever. Amen. (Hebrews 13:20-21)

NOTES:
1. Jean Becker, "We Believe—and We Believe We're Going to Heaven," *USA Weekend Magazine* (December 19, 1986), pages 5-6. [Note: This poll on religious attitudes was based on the interviews of 604 randomly selected adults from across the United States.]
2. Becker, "We Believe," page 5.
3. Becker, "We Believe," pages 5-6.
4. J.I. Packer, *Knowing God* (Downers Grove: InterVarsity Press, 1973), page 209.
5. Louis Berkhof, *Systematic Theology* (Grand Rapids: Eerdmans, 1977), page 77.
6. Packer, *Knowing God*, page 209.

PART III

*Maintaining a
Love Relationship*

CHAPTER ELEVEN

Drifting from Our First Love

*Of all earthly music, that which
reaches farthest into heaven is the
beating of a truly loving heart.*
HENRY WARD BEECHER

It was nearly two years after developing a love relationship with the Lord when I began to notice that something was different in my worship and devotional life. The intensity of my dedication was seemingly growing weaker. Distractions were becoming more and more frequent. And my ministry approach was focusing more on administrative detail.

As a result, my prayer times and quiet times with God were not nearly as rich and edifying to me as they had once been. In fact, I even found myself skipping my quiet times because of an overactive schedule.

Although I sensed what I was doing, internally I justi-fied my actions, telling myself that I was accomplishing

208 / *Maintaining a Love Relationship*

things "for God" through the various programs I was maintaining. If I missed my devotions on a day when I had to
prepare for a Bible study, then my study took the place of my
devotions. If I spent some time praying with the church staff
on a particular day, then that took the place of my own
personal time of prayer. I was compromising my time with
the Lord, substituting my responsibilities to man for my
responsibilities to God.

It was not until a good friend of mine shared some
observations about my spiritual behavior that I realized
how compromising I had become. He said that I was not as
compassionate or forgiving toward weaker Christians as I
had once been. He also said that I seemed less patient, and
that I was becoming more concerned with programs than
with people at committee meetings.

Well, to say the least, his observations disturbed me—
especially since I knew he was right. I was becoming more
dedicated to the task, but my love for God was losing its
intensity. Consequently, my love for the brethren was losing
its sensitivity, and it was becoming obvious to others.

After my friend shared with me, I knew something had
to be done. I knew what the problem was, and yet, perhaps
out of shame, I was afraid to face the Lord with it. But
finally, a couple of days later, I went to my secluded spot in
the mountains and spent several hours alone with Him.
There, through His Word, He gently reminded me of His
never-ending love and His desire for me to draw near to
Him. I asked His forgiveness and then reestablished my
commitment to again walk closely with Him in love.

Suddenly my perspective on everything seemed to
change. The needs of others were again more important
than any planned program or task. My heart felt a renewal
of sensitivity to the Holy Spirit. And my compassion for the
lost regained its zeal. It was not that I had backslidden or fallen

out of love with God but rather that my motivation to keep my eyes constantly fixed on the Lord was weakening as I gave increasing priority to other things. I was becoming rigidly disciplined by trying to accomplish too much, too fast—in the flesh.

Sustaining a love relationship with the Lord takes constant effort on our behalf. But isn't that always the requirement for true *agapē* love? Doesn't it always require time and effort to involve ourselves in a deep love relationship with another person? Why? Because true love demands loyalty and commitment. And loyalty and commitment means a willful decision to remain steadfast through the busiest schedule, through the most painful trial or tempting circumstances. A love that is weak in its steadfast endurance is not really love at all. It is merely a stronger form of appreciation masquerading as love. It produces no sacrificial actions and is fleeting with time. John certainly understood this distinction when he reminded believers that their love was to be put into positive action: "Little children, let us not love with word or with tongue, but in deed and truth" (1 John 3:18).

The church at Ephesus was guilty of losing the initial zeal of their love for the Lord. Read the Lord's own description of this church's problem:

> "I know your deeds and your toil and perseverance, and that you cannot endure evil men, and you put to the test those who call themselves apostles, and they are not, and you found them to be false; and you have perseverance and have endured for My name's sake, and have not grown weary. But I have this against you, that you have left your first love.
>
> "Remember therefore from where you have fallen, and repent and do the deeds you did at first; or

else I am coming to you, and will remove your lamp-stand out of its place—unless you repent." (Revelation 2:2-5)

The church at Ephesus was doing many things right. They worked hard at spreading the gospel; they persevered through persecution; they were great at discerning false prophets. And in all of this they never tired. Yet the Lord brought a very serious indictment against the church: They had forsaken their first love.

Jesus declared earlier that the greatest commandment is to love God with all our heart, soul, mind, and strength (Mark 12:29-30). Therefore, loving God should be *the* top priority for every believer. But the people of the church at Ephesus had drifted from their original devotion to Him. They became preoccupied with theological matters. Not that those matters were unimportant. But the overemphasis placed on them caused the people's love and devotion to God to take a back seat. They became so overly concerned with theological matters that the warm, intimate devotion they once eagerly expressed to God faded into meetings, debates, and theological discussions. And the Lord rebuked them for it.

The church at Ephesus illustrates a very important message to all believers: We must never forget *who* comes first—God Almighty—and *what* comes first—our sincere love and devotion to Him. We must also never attempt to justify the things we "do" for God as a substitute for our personal communication of our love to Him. I am sure the Ephesian Christians felt that everything was fine because they were "doing" everything they thought they were sup-posed to do. But with such a mind-set, it is easy to become preoccupied with duties and subtly lose sight of our rela-tional responsibilities with the Lord and those He has placed around us.

In maintaining a love relationship with the Lord, we must guard against drifting from our most important priority: loving and seeking Him first. We must never permit things that we may do in the name of the Lord to become our *only* means of acknowledging Him. God demands that we acknowledge Him through our love, loyalty, and faithfulness: "For I delight in loyalty rather than sacrifice, and in the knowledge of God rather than burnt offerings" (Hosea 6:6).

How can we detect when we are beginning to drift in our love relationship with the Lord? What characteristics does *agapē* love produce in a person who is in love with God? Let us approach both of these questions from Scripture.

First Corinthians 13 is often referred to as "the love chapter." There Paul presents for us a beautiful picture of what agape love *is,* what it *does,* and what it *does not do.* In order to help us answer our two questions, let us first observe what love does not do, and then look at what love does. We will approach what love *is* in the final chapter of this book, "Walking in Love."

WHAT LOVE DOES NOT DO

Perhaps by first gaining a better understanding of what *agapē* love does *not* do, we can gain a greater awareness of certain human weaknesses that contribute to a subtle separation in the love relationship. These weaknesses, if not kept in check, will reflect behavioral tendencies not characteristic of *agapē* love.

Paul lists for us six specific actions that love does not do. If we commit one of these actions without recognizing a need for repentance, then quite possibly we have begun to drift in our love relationship with God.

1. Love does no wrong to a neighbor (Romans 13:10).
2. Love does not brag (1 Corinthians 13:4).
3. Love does not act unbecomingly (1 Corinthians 13:5).
4. Love does not seek its own (1 Corinthians 13:5).
5. Love does not take into account a wrong suffered (1 Corinthians 13:5).
6. Love does not rejoice in unrighteousness (1 Corinthians 13:6).

(1) *Love does no wrong to a neighbor* (Romans 13:10). Loving one another is a basic principle of the Christian life (John 13:34). It is also a confirmation of our love for God (1 John 4:16). Therefore, purposely doing something harmful against another person would clearly indicate a breakdown in our love for God (John 14:15). After all, how could we stand before God and declare our love to Him after purposely wronging another person? Surely we could not do that in a sincere love relationship.

I remember an incident that vividly demonstrated a Christian's love for God through his interaction with other people. Janet and I had just moved into a new neighborhood. We were anxious to get started in our ministry and to get to know our neighbors. But just a day after we moved in, our two Alaskan Malamute dogs escaped into our neighbor's backyard where there were four cages of rabbits. But these were no ordinary rabbits. They were championship-bred Patagonian rabbits. Well, unfortunately our dogs broke into some of the cages and killed six of these special rabbits.

After hearing the commotion, our neighbor rushed out and corralled our dogs, then walked them back over to our house. Janet and I were surprised to open the door and see our neighbor, whom we had not yet met, standing on our porch holding our two dogs. I immediately felt a rush of anxiety. I knew something was wrong.

After I took the dogs, our neighbor gently shared with us what had happened. Then without waiting for our response, he welcomed us to the neighborhood and invited us over for dinner. Janet and I, to say the least, were overwhelmed by his sense of friendliness. Even though he had just lost six of his prize-winning rabbits to a couple of seemingly uncontrolled dogs, his first response was to clearly display the love of Christ! He had every right to be upset and demand compensation. Yet the matter of his rabbits was only secondary. His first desire was to minister to us in love.

We became good friends and fellowshiped together on numerous occasions. And as long as we were neighbors, the love of Christ was the central binding element of our relationship. Our neighbors walked in a love relationship with the Lord that was immediately noticeable to all. It was displayed constantly in deed and truth.

(2) *Love does not brag* (1 Corinthians 13:4). I once had a Sunday school teacher who would continually boast about his knowledge of Scripture. In fact, each lesson was filled with personal remarks about all of his "in-depth study," as well as the number of books he had used. Even outside the class, he would often enter conversations and immediately give his "spiritual" insights and opinions, whether they were asked for or not. It wasn't long before he gained a reputation of being a braggart, and people began to avoid him and his class.

When I meet Christians like this, I find myself wondering about their relationship with the Lord. They talk plenty about what *they* are doing, without any mention of the Lord. There is a proper way to boast in the Lord, but empty boasting, writes Leon Morris, "is totally incompatible with the Christian way."[1]

The prophet Jeremiah has recorded for us the very thoughts of God regarding what is proper boasting and what is improper:

> Thus says the LORD, "Let not a wise man boast of his wisdom, and let not the mighty man boast of his might, let not a rich man boast of his riches; but let him who boasts boast of this, that he understands and knows Me, that I am the LORD who exercises loving-kindness, justice, and righteousness on earth; for I delight in these things," declares the LORD. (Jeremiah 9:23-24)

The Lord is simply saying, if you are going to brag, brag only that you understand and know Him. But the Lord also knows that the man who truly understands and knows Him will not need to verbally brag about how godly he is; it will be evident in what he does and how he conducts himself.

The believer who is in love with the Lord has no need to brag about anything he has done, because he is far more impressed by the love God has shown him than in the attention he receives from others. As William Barclay has rightly pointed out, "Love is kept humble by the consciousness that it can never offer its loved one a gift which is good enough."[2]

(3) *Love does not act unbecomingly* (1 Corinthians 13:5). Love rejects what is not according to proper form.[3] In other words, true love behaves itself. It is well-mannered, sincere, respectful, and obedient. It does not promote any behavior that is in contrast to the character of God.

One of the finest young men I have had the opportunity to disciple is an individual whose behavior and character vividly reveal his love relationship with God. Erik Westman is one of those unique young men whose intense love for God shrouds his total character with love, humility, and contentment in all situations. I had the privilege to work with Erik while he was finishing up his last two years of college. During one summer, he and I traveled with a youth ministry team to several different states. Though we were on the road for a time and encountered various difficult situations and circumstances, never once did Erik display any other behavior than that of a Christian who was in love with his God.

This is exactly the point that should be stressed. A person who loves the Lord will display a consistent behavior. He will not be sincere one moment, then insincere the next. He will not be humble one moment and arrogant the next. He will not be forgiving now and unforgiving later. Why? Because God's *agapē* love controls that person's life, and His love does not act unbecomingly. Perhaps Lawrence Pearsall Jacks has said it best: "Nobody will know what you mean by saying that 'God is love' unless you act it as well."[4]

(4) *Love does not seek its own* (1 Corinthians 13:5). Love does not selfishly demand its way, its rights, or its wants. Rather, it is only concerned with the welfare of the loved one. This is the epitome of God's love to man: "For God so loved the world, that He gave His only begotten Son, that whoever believes in Him should not perish, but have eternal life" (John 3:16).

We can express such love to others only if we have a heart that has truly experienced it first from God. Our fallen human nature is unable to develop such selfless love on its own. For our basic drive in life is motivated by self-preservation: Perform only what is good for you, and stand for your rights and your place. But "whenever we start thinking about 'our place,' we are drifting away from Christian love."[5]

It has, in many respects, been very educational for Janet and me to watch our young toddler son go through the various stages of emotional and physical growth. Just after Ryan started to walk and experience interaction with other children, he went through a period when he was selfish with things, whether it was with his drinking cup, blanket, or Mommy and Daddy. This selfishness became very evident when Janet began babysitting a little girl who was about the same age as Ryan. When the two got together, the toys between them became a battleground. "Mine!" "Mine!" They would scream at each other as each tried to pull a toy from the other's grip. Each child laid claim to whatever toy he or she wanted at the time.

Watching their actions reminded me of our basic human nature. As adults, when we want something, we may not scream "Mine!" We merely devise more concealed, more sophisticated ways of getting what we want, even when it is at the expense of another person. But this merely amplifies the beautiful reality of the love of God. At our spiritual birth, we become a new creation (2 Corinthians 5:17). We then gain the ability to live a life that is absolutely concerned with the well-being of others before that of ourselves. How? By recognizing and understanding the greatest example of a selfless life in Jesus Christ. It is because of Him that love does not seek its own.

(5) *Love does not take into account a wrong suffered* (1 Corinthians 13:5). I think my parents would strongly agree if I told you that my behavior in grammar school was less than "angelic." There were times when my actions forced my teachers to take some very harsh steps to remind me who was in control of the class. I especially remember Mrs. Moore, my sixth-grade teacher. She had a little black book that she kept in the top right-hand drawer of her desk. Every single time I, or anyone else, would misbehave, she

would calmly mark down the incident, as well as the date it occurred. After a certain number of incidents, she would take action—and boy, did she take action! I learned very quickly what her threshold of tolerance was.

This is exactly what *agapē* love does *not* do. It does not keep, so to speak, a little black book recording all wrongs committed. The Greek verb in 1 Corinthians 13:5, *logizomai*, means "to reckon or take account of."[6] The *New International Version* translates this as a love that "keeps no record of wrongs."

There have been times in my life when I have been blatantly offended and found myself thinking about ideas for aggressive retribution. But after a few hours or even a good night's sleep, the love of God calms my heart and mind against any foolish thoughts provoked out of emotional pride. When such vengeful thoughts are harbored for any length of time, especially if they develop into negative actions, we are in danger of drifting in our love relationship with God. It is very easy to become offended and then store up our grievances. But this should never be the behavior of someone who is in love with the Lord because true love does not take into account a wrong suffered.

(6) *Love does not rejoice in unrighteousness* (1 Corinthians 13:6). Ever find yourself standing with a group of people who were discussing some misfortunes of another person? And as you listened to the gossip, you found yourself wanting to hear more, even with a degree of pleasure? But love does not take any pleasure in seeing things go badly for others. It finds no pleasure in seeing things that are wrong.

Interestingly, we live in a society that says it is not right to find pleasure in the wrongs or hurts of others, yet in practice does just the opposite. Television and newspaper reports feed us the negative news of natural disasters, the misfortunes of others, and the political and personal blunders of our leaders. Most people have an appetite for watching the other guy "swim in his own stew." Perhaps it relieves us of our own blunders and mistakes. But Paul said this is not characteristic of true love, which will never find any pleasure in the misfortunes of others.

If we could more thoroughly obey this elementary command there would be less gossip and more edifying talk in our churches. Paul warned young Timothy to "refuse foolish and ignorant speculations, knowing that they produce quarrels" (2 Timothy 2:23). If we truly love the Lord, slander or gossip about others will not find a platform for listening or conversation in our lives. For *agapē* love does not rejoice in unrighteousness.

WHAT LOVE DOES

After considering what *agapē* love does not do, let us now consider what love really *does*. This will help us understand the characteristics of a person in love with God. If you are continually unwilling to allow love to work within you through one of the principles below, it may suggest that you are drifting from a heart, soul, mind, and strength love relationship with God, or that you have never really committed yourself to a full *agapē* love for God.

1. Love rejoices in truth (1 Corinthians 13:6).
2. Love bears all things (1 Corinthians 13:7).
3. Love believes all things (1 Corinthians 13:7).
4. Love hopes all things (1 Corinthians 13:7).
5. Love endures all things (1 Corinthians 13:7).
6. Love covers a multitude of sins (1 Peter 4:8).
7. Perfect love casts out fear (1 John 4:18).

(1) *Love rejoices in truth* (1 Corinthians 13:6). The concept of truth is an important theme throughout the Bible. It

is related in most cases to God, His Word, or the gospel.

In the Old Testament, Moses referred to the Lord as "the faithful God, who keeps His covenant and His loving-kindness to a thousandth generation with those who love Him and keep His commandments" (Deuteronomy 7:9). Later, Moses recorded the words of God Himself, who declared that He was "abounding in lovingkindness and truth" (Exodus 34:6). In reference to God's Word, the psalm-ist declared, "The sum of Thy word is truth, and every one of Thy righteous ordinances is everlasting" (Psalm 119:160).

The New Testament declares a similar theme. Truth came through Jesus (John 1:17); Jesus spoke of Himself as the truth (John 14:6); Scripture is referred to as truth (John 8:31-32, 2 Corinthians 6:7); and the gospel is referred to as truth (Galatians 2:5). Truth is a characteristic of the very nature of God. Love is concerned with the cause of Christ, and this love is not fully lived out if this truth is not proclaimed.

Truth should be an intricate part of our daily lives. But at times the truth hurts, especially when it reveals some-thing about us that we are not proud of. But Christian love has no desire to hide the truth, in fact it rejoices when truth prevails. In a love relationship with God, truth should be the only alternative. It should be the standard we hold in both our speech and our actions. We cannot truthfully love God while we are living in untruth.

(2) *Love bears all things* (1 Corinthians 13:7). The Greek verb *stegō* in 1 Corinthians 13:7 means "to cover." It implies that love can cover anything. In other words, it can protect us from or stand up against any injustice, insult, or personal disappointment. For example, if we encounter persecution, discrimination, or even personal loss, God's love in us will sustain and strengthen us.

Some friends of ours had to recently bear through a

very difficult situation. The birth of their daughter was somewhat premature, causing some complications in her lungs to develop. For almost three months, this little girl clung to life as various hoses and tubes were attached to her body.

Now that we have experienced the wonderful birth of our son, Ryan, Janet and I couldn't imagine having to leave our son for the first three months of his life in a hospital while he struggled to survive. But this was exactly what our friends had to go through. Yet by their deep love in Jesus Christ, they were able to bear through the experience and act as a powerful testimony to many people, especially to their nonbelieving friends. It was indeed their deep love for God that encouraged and protected them through it all.

(3) *Love believes all things* (1 Corinthians 13:7). Paul was not saying here that love is gullible and easily duped. Rather, he was stating that *agapē* love is a trusting love. Barclay suggests that it has a two-fold aspect:

(1) In relation to God it means that love takes God at His word, and can take every promise which begins "Whosoever" and say, "That means me!" (2) In relation to our fellow men it means that love always believes the best about other people.[7]

Unfortunately for many of us, truly believing in God's Word and faithfully living in response to it is easier said than done. For example, despite His promises for peace and contentment for living day to day in His care, we continue to live riddled with anxiety and fear. Despite His promises to love us and never leave us, we continue to feel lonely and unloved. Our love is not strong enough to motivate us to rely totally on Him. In other words, our love does not yet believe all things.

In relation to other people, we often exhibit a similar tendency. The world has influenced us to believe the worst about people, which lowers our level of trust and loyalty. When our love does not yet believe all things, we are influenced right along with the world to take the critical perspective—right into our churches and Bible studies.

But within a love relationship, our love "believes all things," which now changes our perspective. Not only do we now have a far greater trust in God's Word (because we know Him more intimately), but we also convey a true sense of respect and trust toward our fellowman. We walk by faith in response to God's Word and we offer our fellowman the benefit of the doubt. The fact that *agapē* love influences us to believe all things is one of the most rewarding aspects of the love relationship. When we have this kind of trust, we can truly live what we believe.

(4) *Love hopes all things* (1 Corinthians 13:7). Hope is the view of optimism. When everything seems to be failing, hope sees the dawning of a new day, the light of the future.

Our hope as believers looks toward the future when the Lord will return. Although we must face difficulties and trials until that time, the hope generated by *agapē* love will encourage us through those difficulties.

Without hope we have nothing; with hope we have everything. Charles L. Allen has rightly observed the basis of our hope: "When you say a situation or a person is hopeless, you are slamming the door in the face of God." And Paul declared the giver of hope: "Our Lord Jesus Christ Himself and God our Father . . . has loved us and given us eternal comfort and good hope by grace . . ." (2 Thessalonians 2:16).

Consider now, the following questions to check yourself to see if perhaps you might be failing to allow the hope of God's love to work in your life:

- Do you become easily discouraged when your prayers go seemingly unanswered?
- Do you frequently find yourself critical of your present circumstances at home, church, or work?
- Do you often feel like quitting spiritually when things aren't going your way?

If one of these questions is repeatedly relevant in your life, it may suggest that you have not fully considered or understood what the love of God reveals about hope. If so, consider spending some time alone with the Lord in prayer and draw near to the God of hope. Then get busy reading His Word and drawing the encouragement of Scripture: "For whatever was written in earlier times was written for our instruction, that through perseverance and the encouragement of the Scriptures we might have hope" (Romans 15:4).

(5) *Love endures all things* (1 Corinthians 13:7). Paul used the Greek verb *hypomenō* in this verse, describing endurance as a strong, active steadfastness. A.T. Robertson described this endurance as something that "carries on like a stout-hearted soldier."[8] Such endurance means more than just bearing up under a situation (as in our second principle). It means that endurance will grow and develop stronger through the course of the hardships. The believer who has such an enduring love will not allow the difficulties of the moment to drain him of his commitment and purpose. As he endures the trial, he grows even stronger.

This description of love helps me understand how persecution often strengthens the Church. The stronger the love, the stronger its stand. One of the most profound and influential books I have ever read is *Foxe's Book of Martyrs*. It is the record of hundreds of bold and courageous believers who thoroughly understood what it meant to endure in love. The stories of their persecution and torture unto death reveal how Christians can endure through everything because of their intense love for God.

It was a proven reality to those martyrs that love endures all. Consider two powerful introductory statements from Foxe's book that refer to these bold Christians and their lives:

> Here is self-sacrifice, springing not from pride, but from humility; founded not upon ignorant prejudice, but upon a faith based upon conviction: arising not from hatred or contempt for man, but from the love of God.
>
> The history of Christian martyrdom is, in fact, the history of Christianity itself; for it is in the arena, at the stake, and in the dungeon that the religion of Christ has won its most glorious triumphs.[9]

(6) *Love covers a multitude of sins* (1 Peter 4:8). There are three basic ways to interpret this verse: (a) God's love covers a multitude of our sins. (b) If we truly love others, then God will overlook a multitude of sins in us. (c) *Our* love will overlook the sins of others; in other words, we can forgive the faults of others because of the forgiving grace of God.

I personally favor the last meaning because it seems so close to Proverbs 10:12: "Hatred stirs up strife, but love covers all transgressions." The meaning here is that love does not "stir up" sins or broadcast them.[10]

This kind of love reminds me of the love a mother has for her child. Her love will never cease despite the actions of that child. Even if the child grows up and commits a serious crime, though the mother is not accepting of her child's behavior, she will nonetheless remain strong in her love toward her child.

I remember my parents often reminding me that they loved me and would always love me regardless of what I might do in my life. This has always been a gentle reminder of what a portion of God's love is like for us. When we have a love relationship with God, our love for others will not cease with the first problem. Our love will enable us to look beyond their faults. Not that we will compromise with sin through our love. Rather, in our love we can be forgiving and tolerant.

(7) *Perfect love casts out fear* (1 John 4:18). The meaning of this truth is not too difficult to grasp once you read it in the context of the entire verse. The idea here is that God's perfect love in us will drive out all fear:

> There is no fear in love; but perfect love casts out fear, because fear involves punishment, and the one who fears is not perfected in love. (1 John 4:18)

Here we have a declaration from God that the believer who is involved in a deep love relationship with Him will not experience (a) fear of His judgment, (b) fear from anything in the world, and (c) fear from ever being separated from Him. He also knows that he is safe and secure in the knowledge that whatever sorrow, pain, or loss may come his way, it will only be for his good and for the glory of God. It is from such a mind-set that perfect love casts out fear.

But also recognize that not just any love casts out fear. Rather, it is *perfect* love that casts out fear. Perfect love is *agapē* love, that deep, complete, trusting, selfless, giving love. Anything less will never encourage enough confidence to produce the kind of trust and loyalty a relationship requires to grow and develop. True love for God results in our confidence in Him, thus dispelling all fear.

Consider the following questions. If any of them

directly applies to your life, your love for God may not be strong enough to produce the confidence needed to walk without fear and to trust completely in God and His Word:

- Is it often difficult to make decisions, especially when they could have a marked effect on your future? If so, it may suggest that you fear the wrong decision out of a lack of confidence.

- Do you find yourself neglecting advice or counsel from mature Christians when you are faced with difficult circumstances? Sometimes our fear leads us to a false sense of security by producing a temporary feeling of confidence and pride. In such a situation we refuse assistance because we are afraid of displaying any fear or uncertainty. Especially in this kind of situation, we have a strong tendency to go it alone, even without prayer.

- Do you frequently refuse to involve yourself in church-related activities that may require some teaching or counseling? In recruiting people for positions in the church, I have often found that one of the principal reasons people give for refusing involvement is their lack of confidence in themselves. They absolutely fear the thought of failure or the look of failure. Confidence does not occur overnight, but learning to place complete trust in God to work His perfect will in us can help remove the fear of failure and replace it with the blessings of functioning in the Body of Christ.

What love does and does not do are clear indications of the strength or weakness of our love relationship with God.

226 / Maintaining a Love Relationship

They should become truths ingrained in our heart to warn us of unloving actions and to encourage us toward loving behavior. In our observance of these truths, we can joyfully be imitators of Christ, walking in love (Ephesians 5:2).

NOTES:
1. Leon Morris, *Testaments of Love* (Grand Rapids: Eerdmans, 1981), page 245.
2. William Barclay, *The Letters to the Corinthians* (Philadelphia: Westminster Press, 1975), page 121.
3. Morris, *Testaments of Love*, page 246.
4. Mead, *Encyclopedia of Religious Quotations*, page 280.
5. Barclay, *The Letters to the Corinthians*, page 122.
6. Gaebelein, *Expositor's Bible Commentary*, Volume 10, page 268.
7. Barclay, *The Letters to the Corinthians*, page 123.
8. A.T. Robertson, "The Epistles of Paul," *Word Pictures in the New Testament*, Volume 4 (Nashville: Broadman Press, 1931), page 179.
9. Foxe, *Foxe's Book of Martyrs*, page 5.
10. Gaebelein, *Expositor's Bible Commentary*, Volume 12, page 246.

CHAPTER TWELVE

Guarding Against Distractions

*A soul disengaged from the world
is a heavenly one; and then are we
ready for heaven when our heart is
there before us.*
JOHN NEWTON

Jesus and His disciples often traveled to the village of Bethany, one of the most beautiful and interesting towns in all of Palestine. Lazarus, Mary, Martha, and Simon the leper all lived there. This was also the place from which Jesus began His triumphant entry into Jerusalem.

Once while He was in Bethany, Jesus was invited to have dinner and fellowship at the home of Mary and Martha. Martha was the older of the two and apparently the one in charge. As the hostess, she began to prepare things, but her sister Mary sat listening to Jesus' words. Soon, Martha became annoyed at her younger sister's unwillingness to pitch in and help her with all the preparations. Finally, she

228 / Maintaining a Love Relationship

could not stand it any longer, so she walked up to Jesus with her finger pointed at her sister and said, "Lord, do You not care that my sister has left me to do all the serving alone? Then tell her to help me" (Luke 10:40).

Can you imagine this scene? Here was the Lord comfortably speaking to His disciples and to Mary when all of a sudden an angry Martha interrupts Him and demands that He order her sister Mary to help her with the preparations. I think that if I had been one of the disciples, I would have leaned back and glanced down at the floor. I would have felt awkward and embarrassed. How could anyone speak to Jesus in such a way?

Well, as usual, the Lord's wisdom and insight into Martha's heart allowed Him the opportunity to teach a very important lesson. His response to her has always been one of my favorites: "Martha, Martha, you are worried and bothered about so many things . . ." (Luke 10:41). I can just see our Lord slowly shaking His head and saying, "Martha, Martha." There is almost a touch of humor in the way He begins His response. And probably Martha was realizing the nature of her intrusion and beginning to feel embarrassed and apologetic.

But after admonishing her, Jesus clarified to her and to the rest of the disciples what was really important: "but only a few things are necessary, really only one: for Mary has chosen the good part, which shall not be taken away from her." Here Jesus reminded His disciples to establish their priorities. What "needed" to be done, at least from Martha's perspective, was not of primary importance. Rather, their love and devotion to Him and His Word was to be their first priority. The learning of God's Word and our obedience to it must be our number-one objective.

Though there is no clear explanation about what "the good part" specifically means, the context seems to indicate devotion or worship. If so, Jesus was saying that we must place at the top of our "do list" our devotion and worship of Him. Interestingly, the preceding parable in Luke 10:25-37 describes Jesus' response to a lawyer who asked Him how he could inherit eternal life. The Lord responded by declaring what must head the list of our priorities:

> "You shall love the Lord your God with all your heart, and with all your soul, and with all your strength, and with all your mind; and your neighbor as yourself."
> (Luke 10:27)

Why does the Lord place so much importance on our love and devotion to Him? Well, besides the fact that He is our Creator, He knows that everything that is accomplished in His Name must spring from a motivation of deep love for Him. Whatever is accomplished from any other motivation is merely an act of the flesh that could lead to spiritual burnout. Our motivation to love Him and to be obedient to His commands is our response as we recognize His perfect display of love shown to us through Jesus Christ. Such a motivation will require that we redefine our priorities to make those things that are good secondary to that which is best: our love and devotion toward God.

As a result of the sin nature (which seeks its own way), we cannot remain steadfastly committed to God by any other motivation except that which is prompted by a deep, reverent love for a holy and just God. And our obedience to His Word will demand a sincere and genuine love. John emphasized over and over that true love for God will make itself evident in our obedience to His commands. Such obedience can only result from a heart affected by God's love, for "we love, because He first loved us" (1 John 4:19).

Because we are imperfect and prone to sin, we must be

on guard against becoming distracted from our first priority of loving Him. To do so, we must train ourselves to consciously acknowledge God first in everything: our prayers, our devotion and worship, our thoughts, our goals, our decisions, our conversations, our mealtimes . . . in everything! Our acknowledgment of Him is seen in both our understanding of His desires for us and our willful submission to those desires. In other words, we think and act according to what is proper and glorifying to God. In doing so, we honor Him by putting Him first.

Having an intimate love relationship with God certainly makes it easier to put Him first. But we must still work at training ourselves to keep from being caught up in distractions, just as Martha had been. Paul reminded young Timothy of this training, which Paul referred to as "discipline":

> Discipline yourself for the purpose of godliness; for bodily discipline is only of little profit, but godliness is profitable for all things, since it holds promise for the present life and also for the life to come. (1 Timothy 4:7-8)

Paul was well aware that a believer may profess a love for God but still go astray in his faith (1 Timothy 6:20-21). Even though Timothy's love for God was without question, Paul still reminded him on several occasions to be strong, to fight the good fight, and to be faithful in his commitment to put God first (1 Timothy 1:18; 4:6-7,10,14-16; 6:11-12,20-21; 2 Timothy 1:6,13-14; 2:1-7,15; 3:14; 4:1-5). We, too, must be aware of our vulnerability to becoming sidetracked by worldly distractions. We must heed the words of Peter: "Be of sober spirit, be on the alert. Your adversary, the devil, prowls about like a roaring lion, seeking someone to devour" (1 Peter 5:8).

In the previous chapter, we observed how we can subtly drift in our love for God by manifesting behavior inconsistent with *agapē* love. We learned what true love does and does not do in the character of the believer.

In this chapter, we will not be considering our personal behavior. Rather, we will present some suggestions on disciplining ourselves in our love relationship with God, and we will consider the subtle intrusion of certain influences that may affect that relationship. We will attempt to answer the following questions: How do we discipline ourselves to avoid the distractions that cause us to lose sight of the importance of putting God first? And what specific distractions could prove damaging to our love relationship? First, let us consider our personal discipline.

PRACTICING OUR LOVE FOR GOD

Within all of us lies a never-ending internal conflict. This conflict is not something that rages out of control or drives us to the brink of mental despair. Rather, it is a subtle, yet powerful and influential force. It is a conflict that greatly influences what we do and why we do it. It is the battle between our emotional impulses (what we sense and feel, commonly understood as our heart response) and our analytical impulses (what we objectively and intellectually think in our mind).

This conflict has been labeled by various noted psychologists in a variety of terms. Sigmund Freud applied the terms (rather loosely) "id" (our inherent "feeling" responses) and "ego" (our rational, logical response, which is in touch with reality). Carl Jung referred to the terms "sensation" (the feeling process) and "intuition" (the thinking process). Others have debated the merits of objective versus subjective, empirical versus passion. But very simply, this conflict could be described as the conflict between our heart and our mind—our emotions versus our intellect.

Gordon MacDonald in his excellent book *Ordering Your Private World* makes the point that the mind must be trained to think, to analyze, and to innovate.[1] I suggest that this has some very interesting implications in our ability to love the Lord. For example, my heart (the seat of emotions) may continually generate the need to acknowledge God. But because my mind may think in so many different directions every day in varying degrees of intensity, it can easily become preoccupied with the duties and pressures of everyday living. As a result, it loses sight of its desire to acknowledge God as its top priority. Thus, conflict results when my mind does not heed what my heart suggests I do.

When we become entrenched in such conflict, we are tremendously vulnerable to worldly distractions that may cause us to neglect our daily responsibility of acknowledging God, thereby weakening our desire to deeply love Him. Not that we are then necessarily backsliding or fulfilling the desires of the flesh. Rather, we become detached in our thinking about God just enough to open the door to the desires of the flesh and the influences of the world. Perhaps that was the primary reason why Peter encouraged the believers of his day to discipline their minds for action:

> Gird your minds for action, keep sober in spirit, fix your hope completely on the grace to be brought to you at the revelation of Jesus Christ. (1 Peter 1:13)

Peter understood perhaps better than anyone how a person could become sidetracked in his love for God—even to the point of forsaking Him.

So how do we gird up our minds for action? How can we discipline our intellect to keep in touch with our heart, so to speak, to continue to recognize our "first love" through all the distractions and pressures of everyday life? The great nineteenth-century Scottish evangelist Henry Drummond gives us some of the most workable advice:

> Love is not a thing of enthusiastic emotion. It is a rich, strong, manly, vigorous expression of the whole round Christian character—the Christlike nature in its fullest development. And the constituents of this great character are only to be built up by ceaseless practice.[2]

How do we improve our musical skills? Practice. How do we improve our teaching skills? Practice. Our athletic skills? Practice. And how do we discipline our minds to better guard against worldly distractions and influences? Practice. By practicing our love for God, we will be more inclined to grow up in all aspects of Christ, who is the Head of our faith. "We are to grow up in all aspects into Him, who is the head, even Christ" (Ephesians 4:15). When we practice His love in us, we will grow in maturity in Him.

I remember injuring my elbow in a football game in high school. For three weeks I had to keep my arm from moving, which meant that it had to be wrapped in a sling. After the sling was removed, I was amazed to feel how weak my arm had become. It had taken just three weeks of inactivity to cause my arm to lose a significant amount of strength that it had built up. It was the practice of lifting weights and performing other various activities that had kept my arm strong.

Our practice of drawing near to God on a daily basis is imperative to our spiritual and emotional strength. We need to draw near to His wisdom, guidance, strength, and love for daily support to keep us from depending on our own weak and foolish wisdom. Going for a number of days without any contact with our heavenly Father could easily open the door to distractions, which may draw us away from Him. Eventually we could become double-minded and unstable.

In order for a marriage relationship to grow and develop, each partner must practice a living commitment through daily displays of love and devotion expressed by both word and deed. A marriage will suffer if these expressions become gradually less frequent because of distractions or other "important" commitments. Your responsibility to creatively communicate your love daily to your spouse is a key to a positive, healthy marriage.

As we have observed in previous chapters, developing and maintaining a love relationship with God is not merely a one-time event, but rather a continual occurrence over time. It is a living relationship requiring our ongoing attention. Such personal daily effort is, as it is in a marriage, vital to a growing, healthy love relationship with the Lord.

But the influences of the world and the flesh continually try to dissuade our thoughts from deeply loving God.

Perhaps one of the most devastating examples of such ungodly distractions directly infecting the love and commitment of people for their God was the influence of Canaan on the nation of Israel. Canaan was a region filled with brutal and perverted moral and religious practices, such as infant sacrifices, prostitution, and polytheism. After Israel conquered Canaan, God commanded the victorious army to completely destroy all that was there (Deuteronomy 7:1-6). The people were forbidden to make any covenants with the inhabitants of Canaan in any way, shape, or form.

Then Joshua, the military commander and leader, publicly addressed his military units by tribe, the rulers of the Israelites, and the people themselves. He reminded each group of the primary spiritual responsibility to love

God, as well as the necessity of separating themselves from the twisted, degenerate practices of the inhabitants of Canaan. It was Joshua's final message just before his death. Joshua said to his military units:

> "Be very careful to observe the commandment and the law which Moses the servant of the LORD commanded you, to love the LORD your God and walk in all His ways and keep His commandments and hold fast to Him and serve Him with all your heart and with all your soul." (Joshua 22:5)

He said to the rulers of the Israelites:

> "You are to cling to the LORD your God, as you have done to this day. For the LORD has driven out great and strong nations from before you; and as for you, no man has stood before you to this day. . . . So take diligent heed to yourselves to love the LORD your God." (Joshua 23:8-11)

And he said to the people:

> "Fear the LORD and serve Him in sincerity and truth; and put away the gods which your fathers served beyond the River and in Egypt, and serve the LORD. . . . You are witnesses against yourselves that you have chosen for yourselves the LORD, to serve Him." And they said, "We are witnesses. . . . We will serve the LORD our God and we will obey His voice." (Joshua 24:14,22,24)

But because Israel did not follow through with God's command to completely destroy all that was in Canaan, the people became drawn away and were unable to stick to the Lord's commands. They were influenced away from the things of God due to their toleration of some of the ungodly practices of the Canaanite inhabitants. Much of the subsequent moral and spiritual decline marking the history of Israel during the time of the judges can be directly traced back to this time of Israel's permissiveness toward the degenerate religion and practices of Canaan.[3]

Israel's primary responsibility to practice her love and devotion to God was set aside and became secondary, if at all. The people became far more enamored with their new country, its inhabitants, and its customs and beliefs. This led to an unspiritual, undisciplined nation without a leader and without direction. "In those days there was no king in Israel; everyone did what was right in his own eyes" (Judges 21:25). It has indeed been historically referred to as one of Israel's darkest periods.

It was not until the appearance of Samuel, Israel's final judge, who called the people to a revival of the true worship of the living God, that the people of Israel began to turn back to their first priority of acknowledging Him (1 Samuel 7:3-17).

If we desire to maintain strength in our love relationship with the Lord, then we must heed the example of the nation of Israel, as well as the admonitions from Peter and Paul that teach us to prepare ourselves against ungodly influences and distractions. We must be willing to practice daily our love and devotion to God.

What things can we practice daily to prepare us against ungodly influences and distractions and to strengthen our love relationship with God? Fourteen practical activities are suggested in Chapter 5, "Time Alone with God." It is the commitment of our daily contact with the Lord that serves as our essential practice in loving Him.

Brother Lawrence told a friend how he drove away influences that interrupted his thoughts of God:

> I worshipped Him the oftenest that I could, keeping my mind in His holy presence, and recalling it as often as I found it wandering from Him. I found no small pain in this exercise, and yet I continued in it, notwithstanding all the difficulties that occurred, without troubling or disquieting myself when my mind had wandered involuntarily. I made this my business as much all the day long as at the appointed times of prayer, for at all times, every hour, every minute, even in the height of my business, I drove away from my mind everything that was capable of interrupting my thought of God. Such has been my common practice ever since I entered religion.[4]

Our love and devotion to God must be a powerful desire gripping our entire being. That love must move us to a strength of mind. Then, we can be steadfast and maturing in our love for Him despite what is thrown at us in the world, remembering that "God has not given us a spirit of timidity, but of power and love and discipline" (2 Timothy 1:7).

TWO DISTRACTIONS

Now that we have illustrated the importance of preparing for and shielding ourselves against ungodly influences and distractions originating from the world, let's take a closer look at two of these distractions that could prove, if unchecked, very damaging to our first-love relationship with God: *money* and *prestige*.

Money—All of us are in one way or another affected by money. It greatly influences what we do and how we do it. It also strongly affects our standard of living, and can even direct our personal behavior. Money, like fire, can be a faithful servant but also a fearful master.

The New Testament offers us several lessons on the use and misuse of money (Matthew 6:19-24; Mark 12:41-44; Luke 12:13-21, 16:10-13; 2 Corinthians 8-9; 1 Timothy 6:17-19), as well as the dangers associated with the love of money (Luke 16:13, Colossians 3:5, 1 Timothy 6:10, Hebrews 13:5).

Money in itself is not a harmful agent. Rather, money can produce a certain attitude of greed that distracts us from an *agapē* love for God. This greed is caused by an insatiable thirst to "have" according to our desires, and leads eventually to the love of money.

This thirst to "have" originates in most cases out of the standards and pressures of the environment we choose to live in. For example, if we choose to live in an environment that places a great significance on high standards and abundant living, the accompanying demands may push us to conform to those high standards even at the expense of our relationship with God and His Church. At this point, money becomes the controlling factor in our lives, and everything, including our relationship with God, revolves around it.

Sometimes the thirst to have originates out of a "lack" in what we have. In many cases, what we perceive to be a lack produces a certain amount of insecurity that prompts our desire to accumulate goods. The result is often living over and above our budget. In other words, we try to eat steak on a hot dog income. When this occurs, the pressure for more money forces us to opt for a second or even a third job. And then it is not too long before our time with the Lord in church or in personal devotions takes a back seat to "work."

Now, I am not so much criticizing an individual who

might need to have a second or third job for a period of time. I certainly remember as a young married seminary student how I had to work at a second and third job at times just to make ends meet. But the key difference is that my need for other jobs was not forced by extravagant spending on things we did not need, nor was it a result of high living standards. Rather, it was simply a matter of keeping current on school tuition and expenses, and maintaining our household.

But I believe that when the desire to have unnecessary "wants" causes us to spend less time with the Lord, with our families, and with the family of God, then we have become selfish and greedy. Money is then a distraction to our walk with the Lord. Paul warned Timothy of this very problem when he pointed out that some believers who longed "for it [money] have wandered away from the faith, and pierced themselves with many a pang" (1 Timothy 6:10).

The New Testament gives us three clear reasons why the love of money is a great distraction to our relationship with the Lord:

(1) The love of money (greed) is idolatry.

> Therefore consider the members of your earthly body as dead to immorality, impurity, passion, evil desire, and greed, which amounts to idolatry. (Colossians 3:5)

Greed can be defined as a ruthless disregard for the rights of others in a desire for or seeking after material things.[5] But we are not only disregarding the rights of others when we are greedy, but we are blatantly disregarding God's right to occupy first place in our lives. And we are committing idolatry by essentially worshiping something other than the Lord. He must be our only object of worship.

(2) The love of money is a root of all sorts of evil.

> The love of money is a root of all sorts of evil, and some by longing for it have wandered away from the faith, and pierced themselves with many a pang. (1 Timothy 6:10)

It is not money, but our love for it, that becomes the root of all kinds of evil. This "love" could lead us into any kind of evil once it grasps control of our lives. And once we are involved in any form of evil, we break our fellowship with the Lord.

(3) The love of money makes us discontent.

> Let your way of life be free from the love of money, being content with what you have; for He Himself has said, "I will never desert you, nor will I ever forsake you." (Hebrews 13:5)

In a genuine love relationship with God, we will be absolutely content with the continual presence of the Holy Spirit in our life. Thus we will be content with what we have been given by Him. Not that we will not have a desire every now and then to get a different car or a new set of clothes. But the love of money would breed a continual discontentment, influencing our behavior to the point of negatively affecting our ministry to others and our relationship with God.

These three aspects of the love of money are not only damaging in our relationship with God but also damaging in our witness to nonbelievers. Unfortunately, when one believer is caught violating the biblical use of money, the world points its finger in accusation at every believer or Christian institution.[6] Let us be on guard not to fall prey to the love of money and let us heed the warning of Paul to Timothy:

Flee from these things, you man of God; and pursue after righteousness, godliness, faith, love, perseverance and gentleness. Fight the good fight of faith; take hold of the eternal life to which you were called, and you made the good confession in the presence of many witnesses. (1 Timothy 6:11-12)

Prestige—The dictionary defines prestige as "authority or importance based on past achievements, reputation, or power."[7] In many ways, all of us desire certain amounts of authority and importance. Such feelings make us feel good about ourselves. At the job we want to be respected as a valuable employee. In school we want to be at the top of the class academically or athletically. At home we want to be the best father or mother, husband or wife. And in Sunday school class we would like to be thought of as spiritually wise and knowledgeable. It is quite normal for us to want to strive for excellence within the limits of our God-given abilities.

But serious problems can arise when we become so preoccupied with becoming the best in the field or pursuing the top echelon in the company that we pursue that goal at all costs. What is our motivation? Most likely much of it is the allure of prestige. And why is prestige so attractive? Because it prompts in us a feeling of importance, of being powerful. But more precisely, it makes us feel we are a notch above everyone else.

The scribes and Pharisees in Jesus' time certainly felt religiously prestigious when they broadened their phylacteries and lengthened the tassels of their garments (Matthew 23:5). Phylacteries were small leather cases worn during prayer. One, called a frontlet, was worn on the forehead. Another was worn on the side of the left arm. In these cases were slips containing written passages of the Law (Exodus 13:3-10,11-16; Deuteronomy 6:4-9,

11:3-21), which served as reminders of the Passover and God's deed of delivering Israel from Egypt.

Because of their great desire for recognition, the Pharisees had been in the habit of widening the straps these phylacteries were attached to. This made these cases stand out so that everyone could readily observe how wonderfully devout these men were! Similarly, by lengthening the tassels on their garments, the Pharisees would conspicuously parade their "holy piety" before all men. They loved feeling important and did everything they could to rub it in.

Perhaps the most striking example of their religious prestige was their "love [for] the place of honor at banquets, and the chief seats in the synagogues" (Matthew 23:6). Jesus issued a warning against this very sin:

> "When you are invited by someone to a wedding feast, do not take the place of honor, lest someone more distinguished than you may have been invited by him." (Luke 14:8)

Prestige, if sought after in the flesh, can result in many different negative character traits: pride, vanity, egotism, self-glorification, and partiality. They all have their roots in the attraction of worldly prestige. A believer in a love relationship with the Lord has no room in his heart for such attractions. The moment he makes room for any of them, his love becomes divided.

James wrote about the sin of showing partiality. He warned believers not to have faith in Christ with an attitude of personal favoritism (James 2:1). He gave an example of two men who came into an assembly. One was wearing a gold ring and dressed in fine clothes while the other was dressed in dirty clothes. James pointed out that it is a sin to give special attention to the one wearing the fine clothes because that is a prejudiced distinction between him and the poor man.

It is difficult in our society not to be influenced by worldly prestige. Fine clothes represent an upper-class, prestigious individual; dirty clothes represent a lower-class, unpopular individual. Which kind of individual is more apt to help our reputation or position? Well, the world will always dictate that the more prestigious individual will elevate our position. So we respond in a self-serving manner toward the prestigious individual, hoping to increase our recognition. By doing so, we dishonor the Lord (and the poor individual) by not fulfilling His "royal law":

> If . . . you are fulfilling the royal law, according to the Scripture, "You shall love your neighbor as yourself," you are doing well. But if you show partiality, you are committing sin and are convicted by the law as transgressors. (James 2:8-9)

In a love relationship with the Lord, we have no need to elevate ourselves in the eyes of others. We have no need to brandish ourselves before people in order to gain their favor. For what greater recognition is there than to experience an intimate relationship with the Creator of the universe? If, for some reason, we begin to be attracted by the pull of prestige to the point of changing our behavior and character to reach for it, it might suggest that we are beginning to lose our perspective in our love for God.

In His Sermon on the Mount (Matthew 5:1-7:29), our Lord taught many important and inspirational lessons to His disciples and to the multitudes who had gathered around. I believe one of His most perceptive and remarkable statements came in His discussion on money (Matthew 6:19-24). Relating things that we cherish to our true intentions, He said, "Where your treasure is, there will your heart be also" (Matthew 6:21). What we cherish, what we hold dear in our daily lives, be it money, prestige, reputation, position, family, or God, will be what we truly hold dear in our hearts. That is what will truly motivate us regarding what we do and why we do it.

Some believers will choose to make a lasting commitment to fall in love with the Lord because it is their heartfelt intention to do so. But some believers will simply desire to remain in touch with God with no intentions to draw any closer to Him. Maybe it's because they are fearful of what it will cost them. Or maybe it's because of what that commitment requires in terms of time and effort. Whatever it is, the bottom line is what we truly cherish in our heart. That alone will ultimately decide whether we choose to draw nearer to God or choose to divide our interests by pursuing peripheral attractions.

The choice is ours to make. Do we intend to love the Lord at all costs? Are we willing to ward off any behavior or distractions that tend to draw us away from Him? Or do we walk into the love relationship with weak intentions that will give us a love for God only for a temporary time or until the first difficulties arise? As we make our choice, we need to keep our Lord's words clearly in mind: "Where your treasure is, there will your heart be also."

NOTES:
1. Gordon MacDonald, *Ordering Your Private World* (New York: Oliver-Nelson, 1985), page 92.
2. Henry Drummond, *The Greatest Thing in the World* (Springdale: Whitaker House, 1981), page 39.
3. Gleason L. Archer, Jr., *A Survey of Old Testament Introduction* (Chicago: Moody Press, 1977), page 274.
4. Brother Lawrence, *The Practice of the Presence of God*, page 31.
5. Gaebelein, *The Expositor's Bible Commentary,* Volume 11, page 212.
6. For an excellent study on the biblical use of money, I suggest you read *Your Money Matters* by Malcolm MacGregor, published by Bethany House, 1980.
7. *Funk and Wagnalls Standard Desk Dictionary,* Volume 2 (New York: Funk and Wagnalls, Inc., 1979), page 523.

CHAPTER THIRTEEN

Walking in Love

*Therefore be imitators of God, as
beloved children; and walk in
love.*
EPHESIANS 5:1-2

Of all the courses I took while I was a student at Talbot
Theological Seminary, my classes in Church history are
perhaps my most memorable. It was very inspirational for
me to read the many bold and courageous accounts of the
early Church establishing itself in a hostile society after
Pentecost. It was also exciting to watch how the Church
survived and became even stronger through the Reforma-
tion period. And it was especially encouraging to observe
the Church continue to grow even further despite the influx
of cults and secular philosophies brought on by the so-
called Age of Enlightenment in the eighteenth century.

But another factor that made my Church history

courses exciting was the teacher. Dr. Ronald Rietveld was a part-time faculty member at Talbot, and taught history full-time at a nearby college. Those of us who had the opportunity to sit under his teaching appreciated the enthusiasm he brought to his subject, as well as his pronounced in-love relationship with the Lord. Dr. Rietveld brought a distinct spiritual quality to his classes. He would begin each class session with a genuine time of prayer. It was not uncommon for him to spend the first ten or fifteen minutes preparing our hearts spiritually so that we could further appreciate the significance of Church history—and it worked wonderfully.

One day, Dr. Rietveld announced to us that we would have the special opportunity to meet a well-known godly saint in our class the following week. Without telling us who this person was, he made us promise that we would not openly discuss the matter with other students outside of our specific class. We also had to promise we would not bring anyone else along to class that day (since our class was as full as it was). We all heartily agreed.

Over the next several days, my classmates and I tried to guess among ourselves who this "special" person was going to be. There was certainly a variety of speculation. Soon the day arrived and all of us were anxiously in our seats several minutes before the start of class. At the bell, Dr. Rietveld walked in and, as was his custom, he directed us in a time of prayer. After prayer he had a few of us secure a large, soft chair and place it in the front of our classroom. He then told us that our special guest was going to share with us for a short time, and then allow us an opportunity for questions. By this time, we could hardly stand the suspense. Who was this person!

Finally, the classroom door opened and with assistance from Dr. Rietveld, Corrie Ten Boom walked into our room and sat in that large chair. Well, to say the least, all of us were awestruck. We rose to our feet and applauded Miss Ten Boom—for what seemed like several minutes.

Here was a woman who, by her devout love and faith in God, survived rather miraculously the atrocities of a German concentration camp during World War II. Here was a woman who was considered the greatest female Dutch evangelist of her day. Here was a woman whose books, such as *The Hiding Place, Tramp for the Lord, This Day Is the Lord's,* and *Each New Day,* have been a tremendous source of inspiration and encouragement to thousands upon thousands the world over. Here she was, sitting gracefully in front of us, a living portrait of a life dedicated to walking in a love relationship with God.

Over the next two hours, Corrie related to us many profound stories of faith and commitment—from her childhood days to the present. She spoke softly and in broken English as she responded in conversation to our inquiries with numerous verses from the Psalms and Proverbs. Her love for the Lord and His precious Word was vividly evident in her speech and demeanor. She represented the perfect model of a person who *knew* her God.

Soon she became tired and we had to end our time with her. But before she left, she challenged us to deeply know and love the Lord with all our heart. Then she led us all in a stirring time of prayer. It was one of the most spiritually uplifting times of my young Christian life, a time I will never forget.

Over the years in ministry, I have often reflected back to that day by remembering the wonderful thoughts and impressions that entered my life from that experience. It seems that whenever I personally encounter a trial or difficulty, I am encouraged by remembering back to Corrie's example of faithfulness throughout all of her ordeals.

But also, when I think of walking in love with the Lord,

I think of people like Miss Ten Boom, Dr. Rietveld, and others I have mentioned in this book, whose lives stand as a trophy of a love relationship. By their walk they have proven that all of us can enter into a lasting, intimate love relationship with God—regardless of our environment or circumstances. But in order to do so, we need to establish the commitment in our heart and mind. We must firmly root our intentions to seek the Lord in a first-love relationship, regardless of the costs. If we do so, He will grant us the privilege of drawing near to Him as He draws near to us.

In our aspiration to love Him, let us remember the powerfully motivating words of David in his final message to the people and to Solomon:

> As for you, my son Solomon, know the God of your father, and serve Him with a whole heart and a willing mind; for the LORD searches all hearts, and understands every intent of the thoughts. If you seek Him, He will let you find Him; but, if you forsake Him, He will reject you forever. (1 Chronicles 28:9)

Let us establish our intention to know God well and to walk in love with Him without compromise.

WHAT LOVE IS AND IS NOT

Paul exhorts us, "Be imitators of God, as beloved children; and walk in love, just as Christ also loved you, and gave Himself up for us, an offering and a sacrifice to God as a fragrant aroma" (Ephesians 5:1-2). What Paul is saying is this: Since love is the essence of the nature of God (1 John 4:16), then love must be an essential element of the believer's character. Therefore, in our day-to-day living we ought to display the love of God in all that we do. We should "walk in love."

But what exactly is God's love and how do we walk in it? In Chapter 11, "Drifting from Our First Love," we observed what love does and does not do through our lives. In terms of walking in God's love, let us now consider what love is and what it is not:

- Love is God sending His only begotten Son into the world to be the propitiation for our sins (1 John 4:9-10).
- Love is obeying God's commandments (1 John 5:3).
- Love is patient (1 Corinthians 13:4).
- Love is kind (1 Corinthians 13:4).
- Love is not jealous (1 Corinthians 13:4).
- Love is not arrogant (1 Corinthians 13:4).
- Love is not provoked (1 Corinthians 13:5).

(1) *Love is God sending His only begotten Son into the world to be the propitiation for our sins.* John has given us a most remarkable description of love:

> By this the love of God was manifested in us, that God has sent His only begotten Son into the world so that we might live through Him. In this is love, not that we loved God, but that He loved us and sent His Son to be the propitiation for our sins. (1 John 4:9-10)

Because God is holy and just, He must be propitiated or appeased due to human sin. Yet because His essence is love, He chose to prove His love to mankind by bearing the wounds of sin in order to offer free and absolute pardon from sin. Therefore, the Cross provides the model for what love is all about. Without the Cross, we would not know love—true love—at all. Leon Morris further clarifies how we should view love:

It is only as we see the spotless Son of God crucified, John is saying, that we can see what *agapē* means. It is not a love given to the worthy or to those God charitably assumes to be worthy; it is lavished on sinners. When we see man for what he is, the wrath of God for what it is, and the cross for what it is, then and only then do we see love for what it is.[1]

The Cross is the starting point for all love. God's love revealed from the Cross defines what true love requires: the commitment to sacrifice one's most beloved possession for another's gain.[2] Our Lord exemplified this sacrifice to us by the supreme test of love: "We know love by this, that He laid down His life for us; and we ought to lay down our lives for the brethren" (1 John 3:16).

So then, as believers walking in a love relationship with the Lord, we should experience the ability to give sacrificially and without grief. We should experience freedom from motives that are directed toward self-gain. And we should find great contentment in abiding in His love as we pour it out to our fellowman. A believer cannot fall in love with a loving God without being changed into a loving person.

(2) *Love is obeying God's commandments.* John declared, "For this is the love of God, that we keep His commandments; and His commandments are not burdensome" (1 John 5:3). We should love not simply in word or theory but in action and reality (1 John 3:18). Keeping God's commandments means action. It requires believers to act beyond merely emotions or feelings. We show that we love God when we do what He wants us to do.

So how can true love be recognized? By actions—sacrificial actions. Such concrete commitment is a true barometer of any love relationship. For example, I could tell my wife all day long how much I love her. But if I never do anything to visibly show her my love, my words soon lose credibility in my wife's heart. And a mother could remind her daughter every day that she loves her, but if she never chooses to spend time showing her daughter her love, her words soon become overused and meaningless.

The person who sings the hymn, "Oh How I Love Jesus," yet neglects to read God's Word and communicate love to his neighbor is certainly not showing his love for God but rather his hypocrisy. Our consistent, selfless actions in deeds of love will reveal the true intent of our heart. And such a steady heart can be established only by the love of God.

(3) *Love is patient* (1 Corinthians 13:4). Patience here refers to people and not necessarily to situations or circumstances.[3] People who experience love are tolerant and slow to anger. Someone who possesses *agapē* love will not be overly restless or short with others. Rather, he will exhibit a gentle, patient spirit, even when he is wronged. And without fanfare, he will display a maturity and strength in the Lord that will be comforting to others.

All of us can probably think of various people who exhibit such patient love. Since Janet and I have had our first child, we have become amazed at the amount of tolerance and patient love many teachers of preschool age children seem to freely display. Two such teachers are friends of ours who have been working with small children in our church for a number of years. They seem to express an extraordinary amount of loving patience toward all the children they work with—week after week, year after year.

Interestingly, one of these friends works as a building inspector. Tom's job requires him to go out to construction sites and approve or disapprove new construction. I was once involved in the building trade myself, and I must say that my memories of building inspectors do not include loving patience. Yet Tom continually displays an amazing amount of love and patience toward each child far beyond what is required. He has learned the patience of *agapē* love and applies it directly toward all people, especially little ones.

But it should be pointed out that patience is not necessarily achieved overnight. In fact, Scripture seems to indicate that much of our patience is learned over the course of time (Romans 5:3, Colossians 1:10-11, James 1:3).

To give you a better indication of how much loving patience you are currently applying in your life, consider the following questions:

- Are you restless in your spiritual life? That is, do you have difficulty waiting patiently on the Lord and perhaps even desire to run ahead of Him? (Psalm 37:7).
- Do you tend to feel overly anxious and impatient in times of trials and difficulties, causing you to seek quick solutions or to look for the easiest way out? (Romans 5:3, 12:12).
- Are you impatient with nonbelievers you are praying for when they continue to refuse to see their need for the Lord? Do you easily give up hope for them? (2 Peter 3:9).
- Are you impatient with the weaknesses of other Christians to the point of developing strong feelings of frustration or intolerance? (Romans 15:1-4).

I would suggest that if any of these questions are conspicuously true in your life, you should consider seeking the Lord's direction. Ask Him to help you begin to take the necessary steps to strengthen the patience that is available to you—both for His glory and your testimony. The measure of patience in the life of a believer who is walking in love with God can clearly be distinguished from the shortage of patience in those believers who are not.

(4) *Love is kind* (1 Corinthians 13:4). The Greek verb *chrēsteuomai,* in this verse translated "kind," is not found anywhere else in the New Testament. The word may have been coined by Paul himself.[4] It seems to refer to a pure kindness, a genuinely gracious behavior.

All of this seems to suggest that Paul was attempting to communicate that God's love in a believer will cause him to be more than just "good." Rather, he will be thoroughly kind, with a spirit of genuine kindness throughout his entire character.

You see, a believer can display kindness on the surface, but still possess a critical, even selfish character within. But the kindness produced by God's love will create an unquestionable tenderness in a person's behavior. He will respond to others from the kindness of his heart—without ulterior motives. He will be considerate and well-meaning in his actions. In an uncharitable, unsympathetic world, he will be God's tool to draw people unto Him. The kindness of God displaying itself in the lives of believers in love with Him inevitably touches the hearts of people.

(5) *Love is not jealous* (1 Corinthians 13:4). *Agapē* love is neither jealous nor envious. It is not prompted to selfishness or greed by the gains or possessions of others. A believer in love with God will be content and even pleased when others are successful. It is unfortunately a part of our fallen nature to covet another's possessions or successes, but the love of God neutralizes and overshadows those desires by causing us to be content in Him.

It was this same contentment that allowed Paul to boldly depreciate things he once cherished in his life:

I count all things to be loss in view of the surpassing value of knowing Christ Jesus my Lord, for whom I have suffered the loss of all things, and count them but rubbish in order that I may gain Christ. (Philippians 3:8)

Several verses later, Paul adds, "Not that I speak from want; for I have learned to be content in whatever circumstances I am" (Philippians 4:11). Paul could declare his contentment because he was secure in his love relationship with the Lord. He truly understood what it meant to walk in love.

For the believer who is walking in love with God, there is no place for jealousy. Yet, if we are honest with ourselves, most of us would have to admit to having struggles with jealousy every now and then.

Often two young people will share with me that they are in love with each other and that they would like my premarital counsel for their relationship. Among other things, I ask such a couple to review together the principles of true love listed in 1 Corinthians 13. I ask them to choose two of these seven principles: one that they consider to be evident in their relationship and another that has been the most difficult for them to live out. Invariably, jealousy is the principle that gives couples the most problems.

Jealousy is difficult to live with. If not controlled and replaced, it often builds up and erupts into emotional displays of anger and strife. James said, "Where jealousy and selfish ambition exist, there is disorder and every evil thing" (James 3:16). Certainly, there is no hint of such behavior in the love of God.

(6) *Love is not arrogant* (1 Corinthians 13:4). Here the Greek word translated "arrogant" is *phusioō*, which means "puffed up with pride."[5] Thus we can say that love is not puffed up with pride. Or, as Barclay puts it, "Love is not

inflated with its own importance."⁶

Love and pride are in direct opposition. They cannot rightly coexist. Though there are many forms of pride, being "puffed up" with one's own importance directly violates the sovereignty of God. For example, though a believer may claim that he is experiencing a deep love relationship with the Lord, if he is "puffed up," he will tend to trust his own wisdom and knowledge before seeking the Lord's direction in prayer. His love for God is just not strong enough to remind him to trust in the Lord first:

> Trust in the LORD with all your heart, and do not lean on your own understanding. In all your ways acknowledge Him, and He will make your paths straight. (Proverbs 3:5-6)

Perhaps one of the most visible signs of *agapē* love in the believer is a character free of arrogance. Many times, a believer's true spiritual condition can be observed by noting his character: Is he humble or is he tainted with arrogance? The believer walking in love with God will be humble in nature yet active in expression. He will be ready to freely give of himself, whereas arrogance only seeks to assert itself.

(7) *Love is not provoked* (1 Corinthians 13:5). Love is not touchy, irritable, or prone to "fly off the handle." A believer infused with such love will not become exasperated with people. He will exhibit a gentle, patient disposition, handling frustrations in stride.

The ability to control one's temper does not develop overnight. True, we have the capacity to control our temper once we experience and manifest the love of God. But we must still work at replacing our tendency to seek revenge when we have been unfairly wronged. John is a good example here for us to observe. He developed his self-control over the course of time.

Once when Jesus and the disciples were heading toward Jerusalem, they were denied a place to stay in a Samaritan village. At that time, John, who is now referred to as the apostle of love, immediately wanted Jesus to bomb the villagers with fire from heaven! (Luke 9:54). But the Lord rebuked him for his anger: "You do not know what kind of spirit you are of. For the Son of Man did not come to destroy men's lives, but to save them" (Luke 9:55-56). Later in his ministry, this same angry, impulsive disciple would be used by God to pen perhaps the greatest book on love ever written.

Throughout John's first Epistle, words and expressions such as "walk in the light," "beloved," "little children," and "love one another" clearly illustrate the patient maturity of the love of God that had eventually gripped John's character. But it had not yet rooted itself within him back when he was traveling with Jesus. It took time for John to allow the patience of *agapē* love to control his life.

All of us every now and then become angry. But when that anger becomes malicious, our flesh begins to control our love and behavior.

There are three considerations we should keep in mind when we try to determine whether or not God's love is in control when we become angry. (a) Have we been provoked because our rights or the rights of another have been violated? If it were our rights, chances are we would be more inclined emotionally to seek retribution, which could very easily lead to sin (Ephesians 4:26). (b) Is our anger justified? Most likely, the more it is justified, the more difficult it will be to confess. (c) How long do we hold on to our anger? The Bible warns us against allowing anger to occupy our thoughts for more than a day: "Be angry, and yet do not sin;

do not let the sun go down on your anger" (Ephesians 4:26).

Walking in love with God is our best protection against a fiery temper, for it is then the love of Christ that controls us (2 Corinthians 5:14).

LOVING OUR NEIGHBOR

Let us now shift our thinking to a very key aspect of walking in love with God. According to Christ, our love for others is closely tied to our love for God (Matthew 22:34-40, Luke 10:25-37, 1 John 5:2). But should our love for others be given mainly to believers, or should it be shown to all people? Let's consider each position.

There are some who say that the New Testament teaches that we are to love only those within the Body of Christ (John Knox, Hugh Montefiore, J.N. Sanders, and E. Kasemann). Their claim, among others, is essentially founded on the apparent observation that John's writings refer only to the love of the brethren.[7]

But then there are the many Bible verses that refer to loving our "neighbor" (Matthew 5:43, 19:19, 22:39; Mark 12:31,33; Luke 10:27; John 13:34; Romans 13:9-10; Galatians 5:14; James 2:8). The question here must be, "Who is our neighbor?" This was exactly the question a certain lawyer asked Jesus. Our Lord responded in parable form that *everyone* is our neighbor (Luke 10:29-37).

Further, there are several passages that clearly refer to the Lord Jesus Christ's love for all men, not just for believers: in His sacrificial death (John 3:16, Romans 5:8); in His appearance (Titus 3:4); and in His prayer for the world (John 17:23). After meeting Zaccheus in Jericho, Jesus defined the whole point of His love: "The Son of Man has come to seek and to save that which was lost" [all men] (Luke 19:10).

It should be clear from Christ's example that our love

(which, for believers, is God's love working through us) is to be expressed to all people, not just to those inside the Church. Why would God, who loved the world enough to send His only Son to sacrificially die for all our sins, want us to confine our love merely to believers? It would seem to be contrary to the very nature of God, who is indeed love (1 John 4:16).

The biblical principle of loving everyone does not need to be stressed to most Christians. However, I have found believers who seem to live their Christian lives as though every nonbeliever is their enemy or rival. It's not that they consciously declare their refusal to show love to the nonbeliever, but they demonstrate it in their actions. Whether they neglect to help the poor and indigent or refuse all contacts with the world, these believers communicate a lack of *agapē* love to those who have not yet trusted Christ. They are like the priest and the Levite in our Lord's parable, who refused to help the injured man on the road to Jericho. Let us take extreme caution against ever giving such a heartless impression, especially if we openly claim to have a love relationship with God. Let us make sure we practice what we believe so that we can truly be a light to a darkened world.

Unfortunately, it is very easy for us to get comfortable and even become secluded in our own little Christian environment. Such an isolationist lifestyle comes across as snooty self-righteousness to the rest of the world. Let us not forget the words of Paul to Titus:

> In all things show yourself to be an example of good deeds, with purity in doctrine, dignified, sound in speech which is beyond reproach, in order that the opponent may be put to shame, having nothing bad to say about us. (Titus 2:7-8)

There should be no doubt that walking in a love relationship with God will result in a sincere display of love to everyone we come in contact with. And this includes our enemies, as well as our brethren in Christ (Matthew 5:44; Luke 6:27,35). Let's not forget Jesus' rhetorical question: "For if you love those who love you, what reward have you?" (Matthew 5:46).

LOVING THE BRETHREN

Now regarding the Body of Christ, the New Testament seems to place a heavy emphasis on the importance of loving other Christians. There are at least twenty-three examples of the verb *agapaō* that convey the idea of love within the Christian family.[8]

Perhaps the clearest admonition is given to us in Peter's first Epistle:

> Since you have in obedience to the truth purified your souls for a sincere love of the brethren, fervently love one another from the heart. (1 Peter 1:22)

Love for nonbelievers is not in view here. Rather, Peter is speaking to believers who, because of placing their trust in Christ, have been cleansed from sin. And because they have been purified, Peter exhorts them to love their fellow believers from a fervent, pure heart. So in the case of a believer in love with God, he will also walk in an attitude of love with his fellow believer. If this is not true, then he is a liar and does not truly love God:

> If some one says, "I love God," and hates his brother, he is a liar; for the one who does not love his brother whom he has seen, cannot love God whom he has not seen. (1 John 4:20)

In many ways, John's admonition is perhaps one of the most widely violated principles in Christianity today. Denominational lines define our limits of love; doctrinal positions establish how we love; and social habits decide who we love. But the message of Christ *is* love—impartially and sacrificially displayed to all. Let His example be our only guide. Observe just a few examples of what Scripture loudly declares. Jesus pronounced:

> "A new commandment I give to you, that you love one another, even as I have loved you, that you also love one another." (John 13:34)

> "Just as the Father has loved Me, I have also loved you; abide in My love." (John 15:9)

Paul affirmed:

> I have been crucified with Christ; and it is no longer I who live, but Christ lives in me; and the life which I now live in the flesh I live by faith in the Son of God, who loved me, and delivered Himself up for me. (Galatians 2:20)

And John echoed:

> We know love by this, that He laid down His life for us; and we ought to lay down our lives for the brethren. (1 John 3:16)

There can be no question about it. Christ's love is our supreme example for our love for one another in the Body of Christ. In Him we find the unifying element for our faith: "For in Christ Jesus neither circumcision nor uncircumcision means anything, but faith working through love" (Galatians 5:6). There is, then, no real love outside of Christ.

* * *

Seeking and establishing a love relationship with God is the greatest experience a believer can achieve in his lifetime. It is the profound opportunity to draw near to our God and Creator, who chose to create us in His image. And it is our great chance to more deeply appreciate the vastness of His love as we grow in the knowledge of His ways.

Martin Luther made a very powerful observation about how man loves:

> Whatever a man loves, that is his god. For he carries it in his heart; he goes about with it night and day; he sleeps and wakes with it, be it what it may—wealth or self, pleasure or renown.

If what we choose to love is God, then He will be our God. We will carry Him in our heart and will honor Him in our ways. So let us choose to fall in love with God. And let our love be faithful and true, for God delights in unchanging love (Micah 7:18). And in our love, let us remember Jude's closing exhortation to the Christians of his day, that we are to keep ourselves "in the love of God, waiting anxiously for the mercy of our Lord Jesus Christ to eternal life" (Jude 21).

NOTES:
1. Leon Morris, *Testaments of Love*, page 131.
2. Gaebelein, *Expositor's Bible Commentary*, Volume 12, page 343.
3. Barclay, *The Letters to the Corinthians*, page 119.
4. Robertson, *Word Pictures in the New Testament*, Volume 4, page 177.
5. Vine, *Expository Dictionary of New Testament Words*, page 230.
6. Barclay, *The Letters to the Corinthians*, page 121.
7. Morris, *Testaments of Love*, page 211.
8. Morris, *Testaments of Love*, page 204.